MW01125264

ON THE ROCKS

The brain goes through dynamic changes during adolescence. Alcohol can damage both short- and long-term growth processes.	921	07659611	750 ml
TEENS AND ALCOHOL	**BY** *David Aretha*		

TEENS AND ALCOHOL

Please note: All information is as up-to-date as possible at the time of publication.

Photographs © 2007: age fotostock: 52 (Dennis McDonald), 85 (PhotoDisc); Alamy Images: 98 (Werner Dieterich), 94 (Peter Horree); AP/Wide World Photos: 112 (Craig Line), 120 (Darrin Phegley, The Hawk Eye), 67 (Gregory Smith); Bridgeman Art Library International Ltd., London/New York: 19 (Atwater Kent Museum of Philadelphia/Courtesy of Historical Society of Pennsylvania Collection); Corbis Images: 91 (Randy Faris), 68 (Rick Gomez), 25 (Hutchings Stock Photography), 104 (Michael Kim), 63 (Tom & Dee Ann McCarthy), 58 (Roy Morsch/zefa), 6 (Richard T. Nowitz), 79, 80, 88 (Mark Peterson), 107 (Fred Prouser/Reuters), cover inset, 1 (Royalty-Free), 60 (Ariel Skelley), 76 (Paul A. Souders), 70 (David H. Wells); Envision Stock Photography Inc./Reso: 44; Getty Images: 123 (Barros & Barros/The Image Bank), 42 (Mary Kate Denny/Stone), 54 (Ed Freeman/The Image Bank), 10, 32 (Zigy Kaluzny/Stone), 22 (Eric O'Connell/Taxi), 5 (Barbara Peacock/Taxi), 40, 103 (Photodisc Green), 74 (Taxi), 96 (VCL/Taxi), 15 (David Young-Wolff/Stone); JupiterImages/BananaStock: 57; Kathy Petelinsek: cover, 1; Photo Researchers, NY/Larry Mulvehill: 114; PhotoEdit: 64 (Lon C. Diehl), 37 (Myrleen Ferguson Cate), 28 (Tony Freeman), 8, 39 (Spencer Grant), 34 (Michael Newman), 47 (Dana White); PictureQuest/Image Source: 16; Superstock, Inc.: 82, 87 (BananaStock), 20 (Culver Pictures, Inc.); The Image Works: 100 (Drew Crawford), 117 (Sven Doering/Visum), 24 (Mark Reinstein), 119 (Jim West); Tom Keck Photography: 30.

Book design by The Design Lab

Library of Congress Cataloging-in-Publication Data
Aretha, David.
  On the rocks : teens and alcohol / by David Aretha.
    p. cm.
  Includes bibliographical references and index.
  ISBN-10: 0-531-16792-5 (lib. bdg.)   0-531-17976-1 (pbk.)
  ISBN-13: 978-0-531-16792-2 (lib. bdg.)   978-0-531-17976-5 (pbk.)
  1. Youth—Alcohol use—United States—Juvenile literature. I. Title.
  HV5135.A74 2006
  613.81—dc22   2005024291

Copyright © 2007 David Aretha.
All rights reserved. Published in 2007 by Franklin Watts,
an imprint of Scholastic Library Publishing.
Published simultaneously in Canada.
Printed in Mexico.

FRANKLIN WATTS and associated logos are trademarks and/or registered trademarks of Scholastic Library Publishing. SCHOLASTIC and associated logos are trademarks and/or registered trademarks of Scholastic Inc.

1 2 3 4 5 6 7 8 9 10 R 16 15 14 13 12 11 10 09 08 07

Cor. of Fifth & Chestnut St

ON THE ROCKS

The brain goes through dynamic changes during adolescence. Alcohol can damage both short- and long-term growth processes.	**921**	07659611	750 ml
TEENS AND ALCOHOL	**BY** *David Aretha*		

Franklin Watts®

A Division of Scholastic Inc.
New York • Toronto • London • Auckland • Sydney
Mexico City • New Delhi • Hong Kong
Danbury, Connecticut

Contents

Forget any stereotypes you have about alcoholics.
Alcoholism affects people of all ages and genders.

1 | Getting Started

"I cannot tell you my first bubble gum, pizza or ice cream, but I can tell you my first drink. . . What I remember most is that it ran out far too quickly."

[—recovering alcoholic]

Cindy knew what an alcoholic looked like. Male. Late sixties. Slept on park benches and drank from a bottle wrapped in a grimy, brown paper bag. Smelled like last week's trash. Drank so much that he lost his job, his family, and his future. Begged for money so he could make it to his next sip.

Then Cindy looked in the mirror. She was a fourteen-year-old Houston girl with practically her whole life in front of her. And it occurred to her that an alcoholic did not look anything like her preconceived image.

Loss of memory is just one of the adverse effects of alcohol abuse.

CHUGGING AT THREE

Cindy's father had introduced her to alcohol at age three. Harmless fun. You know, sips of beer at first. Then Cindy got to the point where she would chug down half a bottle and make the adults laugh when she staggered and fell flat on her face.

Three years old, and she had discovered how drinking beer helped her "fit in" with adults. By age five, she was allowed to finish a bottle or two. She learned to sneak extras, even hiding beer in the thermos she brought to school with her lunch.

Cindy recalls "getting bombed" in third grade. By fifth grade, she would get the shakes if she went too long without alcohol. Already she was addicted. Sixth grade was a big year for Cindy. She made friends who shared her love of drinking. She became "loud, rude, and obnoxious."

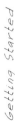

Her parents separated. Alcohol numbed her pain. She was suspended from school and busted for shoplifting. Again, alcohol numbed the pain. When it was not enough, she tried drugs, eventually becoming addicted to them as well.

A LOST DAY

Cindy didn't realize that she had a problem until after a particular day. She recalls swallowing a lot of pills. She had strange visions and began pulling out her hair. The next day, when her friends commented on what a great time she had had at a gathering, she could not remember attending.

Feeling down, but not yet admitting she had a problem, Cindy turned to a friend who convinced her to enroll in a twelve-step **rehabilitation** program. She tried it, liked it, and stayed straight for a while. But after a move to Colorado, Cindy returned to drinking and drug use.

HELP AT LAST

Now desperate, Cindy called **Alcoholics Anonymous (AA)**. One of the program's leaders took an interest in her, and the two decided to start a teenage AA group. They talked alone for the first few months. Finally, someone else came for help, and the group grew quickly after that.

The number of teenagers seeking treatment for alcohol abuse continues to increase every year.

That was when Cindy realized that all her stereotypes about **alcoholism** and alcoholics were just that—stereotypes. She learned in the hardest way imaginable that an alcoholic can be a fourteen-year-old girl just as easily as a smelly old man on a park bench.

SOBER—AND FREE

At seventeen, Cindy had been **sober** for three years. She has painful memories of her school years—years that were supposed to be among the best in her life. She also feels satisfaction in knowing that her insight may help others in their recovery. She no longer feels like a prisoner of the liquor she began enjoying at such an early age.[1]

FIVE MILLION ABUSERS

While youth drug use has fluctuated over the years, several studies indicate that alcohol use among teenagers remained steady from the mid-1900s to about 2005.[2] This does not mean, however, that underage drinking is not a major problem among American youths.

Many teens are entering **alcohol abuse** treatment programs, and their number is growing rapidly. Those teens are taking a step in the right direction. But for every teen starting treatment, experts can only guess at the number who should be doing the same. The National Institute on Alcohol Abuse and Alcoholism (NIAAA) estimates that more than 5 million American teenagers are alcohol abusers.

Cindy is one of the lucky ones—and one of the rare teens to recognize her problem so young. Though she thought that she fit in with other drinkers her age, she could never relate to kids who did not use alcohol or drugs, and it bothered her. She became increasingly lonely as her highs became more frequent.

As of 2000, about **250,000 teenagers were entering alcohol abuse treatment** programs every year.[3]

- About **67% of 13-year-olds** say they have used alcohol.

- In one survey of teen alcoholics, **88% said they began drinking before they were 10.**[4]

CHOICES

Cindy has learned to make better choices, but she needs the support of her teenage AA group. This works out perfectly because she reaches out to others who need the meetings, too.

There are many people and programs out there trying to slow underage drinking before alcohol tears apart more lives. Many of them are highly successful. But even if a program helps only one youth in the struggle to live a sober life, that's a success.

The widespread study of teenage alcoholism in the United States is fairly recent. Alcoholism used to be considered mainly an adult issue.

Now, alcohol studies are aimed at younger and younger age groups, and with ample reason. Statistics from the Centers for Disease Control and Prevention (CDC) show that in 2003, nearly 28 percent of U.S. students reported that their first drink of alcohol, other than a few sips, came before age thirteen.[5] By the mid- to late teens, the prevalence of alcohol use rises sharply.

GOOD NEWS

For students who choose sobriety, there is good news. According to Joseph A. Califano Jr., former U.S. secretary of Health, Education, and Welfare and founder of the National Center on Addiction and Substance Abuse (CASA) at Columbia University, "a child who reaches age twenty-one without smoking, abusing alcohol, or using drugs is virtually certain never to do so."[6]

TEEN ALCOHOL TRENDS

- About **80%** of high-school seniors have **used alcohol.**

- Almost **30%** of high-school seniors **abuse alcohol.**[7]

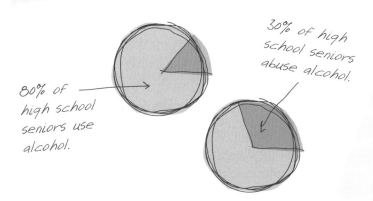

80% of high school seniors use alcohol.

30% of high school seniors abuse alcohol.

A University of Michigan study surveys some 50,000 students each year. The percentage of students in a recent survey who reported having consumed alcohol (more than a few sips) is listed below:

- **8th-graders 44%**
- **10th-graders 64%**
- **12th-graders 77%**[8]

The best way for teens to avoid alcohol problems later is to stay away from alcohol altogether. But only a minority of today's teens make that choice. So programs are needed to help keep alcohol from becoming a problem for those who do try it. Such programs need to recognize the basic tendencies of young alcohol users.

DEMOGRAPHIC TRENDS

Alcohol makes no distinctions. Young people of all races, creeds, and backgrounds can develop alcohol problems once they start drinking. However, the University of Michigan's Monitoring the Future (MTF) study uncovered some interesting trends regarding underage drinking.

Adolescents who begin drinking before age 15 are four times more likely to become dependent on alcohol than those who wait until the legal age of 21.
—NIAAA[9]

Statistically, African American youths are less likely to abuse alcohol than White youths.

White youths typically used the most alcohol, followed closely by Hispanics. African Americans had significantly lower levels of alcohol use across all age groups studied, by more than half in some instances. Geographic differences were slight.[10]

- The average age when **boys first try alcohol: 11**

- The average age when **girls first try alcohol: 13**

- The average age when **Americans begin drinking regularly: 15.9**[11]

Girls and boys are almost equally likely to use alcohol.

Gender differences have fluctuated more than ethnic differences over the years. In fact, some researchers have suggested that the differences in alcohol use among girls and boys have been disappearing recently—that each gender is just as likely to drink before age twenty-one. However, the MTF research finds some differences.

Binge drinking and drinking during a two-week period were significantly higher among twelfth-grade boys than among girls the same age in the Michigan study. Dr. Michael Windle, professor of psychology and director of the Center for the Advancement of Youth Health at the University of Alabama at Birmingham, concludes that "although alcohol use and dangerous drinking practices (e.g., getting drunk, binge drinking) occur among both boys and girls, these practices are more prevalent among boys by the twelfth grade."[12]

Alcohol abuse is a danger for any young person who drinks. Both sexes and all races are vulnerable.

In one study of 12th-graders,

- **52% of boys** reported using alcohol in the last 30 days

- **34% of boys** said they got drunk during that time

- **45% of girls** reported using alcohol in the last 30 days

- **27% of girls** said they got drunk during that time. (MTF)[13]

ALCOHOL THROUGH THE AGES . . .

Alcohol has been around since long before humans existed. It is produced naturally in plant materials. Almost all fruits, grains, and vegetables contain energy-rich sugars. Those sugars are broken down by microscopic yeast spores in a process called **fermentation**. During fermentation, the sugars are transformed into alcohol and carbon dioxide.[14]

Fermentation can occur naturally, so prehistoric birds and animals may have felt the effects of drunkenness. How humans happened onto fermentation is something of a mystery.

One legend holds that, about five thousand years ago, King Dshemshid of Persia (now Iran) was so fond of grapes that he ordered his servants to store large jars of them.

Months later, the skins had burst and the jars contained only a dark purple juice. On his orders, the jars were labeled "poison" and stored in the cellar, until a woman suffering from terrible headaches decided to kill herself.

You can probably guess the rest. The woman drank from the "poison" in an effort to end her life. Instead of dying, though, she felt better. When she told the king what had happened, he too tried the liquid and enjoyed its effects. King Dshemshid decided to set aside some of each year's grape harvest for making this juice, which he called royal medicine.[15] We call it wine.

. . . AND AROUND THE WORLD

Historians speculate that prehistoric nomads learned to make a form of beer from grain and water before they learned to make bread. Clay tablets from ancient Babylonia (in today's Iraq), dating from 4300 B.C., contain beer recipes.[16]

The ancient Chinese made a beer called kiu from millet and rice. Beer was especially popular with northern Europeans, whose climate was too cold to grow grapes for wine. In ancient Egypt, beer was used as a religious offering and was sometimes buried in royal tombs.

A **father's warning** to his son about the **dangers of drinking too much beer** was discovered in Egyptian writings more than 4,000 years old.[17]

Engel and Wolf's Brewery was one of many breweries to bring the German style of beer to American drinkers in the late 1800s.

AMERICANS AND BEER

By the time Europeans came to the New World, alcohol had long been a staple of many of the settlers' diets. Harvard College had its own brew house in 1674. William Penn, the founder of Pennsylvania, opened his own commercial brewery in the 1680s. In 1757, George Washington wrote out his personal beer-making recipe. Drunkenness, however, often led to public punishment.

German immigrant brewers in the 1850s added to America's beer offerings, and by the late 1800s there were more than two thousand breweries in the United States. Clearly, many Americans enjoyed their beer.

The outlawing of alcohol in 1919 led to years of illegal alcohol production.

TEMPERANCE AND PROHIBITION

Others saw alcohol as evil and tried to outlaw it. In the early 1800s, many **temperance** movements sprang up in the United States. These were organized efforts to require citizens to abstain from alcohol. Among the more success-ful groups was the Woman's Christian Temperance Union (WCTU), founded in 1874.

Some temperance groups pushed to outlaw alcohol consumption and sales, but most of these efforts failed. The WCTU, however, along with the Anti-Saloon League (founded in 1895), built considerable political power and demanded governmental control of alcohol. **Prohibition** soon became widespread, ushering in a controversial period in U.S. history.

Laws regulating drinking were enacted during World War I (1914-1918), when conservation policies limited alcohol output. Then, in 1919, the Eighteenth Amendment to the U.S. Constitution, prohibiting the manufacture, sale, import or export of intoxicating liquors, was ratified. The 1919 Volstead Act—officially, the National Prohibition Act of 1919—made provisions for that amendment to be enforced. It also gave federal agents the power to investigate and prosecute violations.

What followed was the largest period of illegal drinking in U.S. history. Enforcing the Prohibition laws proved to be impossible. Alcoholic beverages were being concocted all over the country, sometimes with dangerous ingredients or brewing methods. Large-scale smuggling, called bootlegging, could not be prevented, nor could the consumption of "moonshine," homemade liquor. To keep prohibitionists from catching on, people gave their illegal brews such nicknames as white lightning, skull cracker, bush whiskey, stumphole, and tiger's sweat.

Mother's in the kitchen, washing out the jugs;
Sister's in the pantry, bottling the suds;
Father's in the cellar, mixing up the hops;
Johnny's on the front porch, watching for the cops.
—Prohibition-era song[18]

One way to prevent drunk driving is to collect the keys of everyone drinking at a party.

REPEAL

In 1933, the Twenty-first Amendment repealed Prohibition on a national level. Some states and counties kept their Prohibition laws on the books, but to no avail. Alcohol consumption was not going away, and by 1966 there were no such laws remaining.[19]

Recent U.S. laws restricting the consumption of alcohol have focused on young people. As recently as the early 1980s, some states allowed eighteen-year-olds to drink. But under the 1984 National Minimum Drinking Age Act, states that refused to raise the legal age for purchase and possession of alcohol could lose federal highway funds. By 1988, all fifty states had a drinking age of twenty-one.

40% of all **traffic-related deaths** in 2003 occurred in **alcohol-related crashes.**[20]

ALCOHOL AND DRIVING: A DANGEROUS MIX

Drinking and driving do not mix. It's a cliché. It's an advertising slogan. It's also one of the most important facts for any drinker to remember.

The National Highway Traffic Safety Administration (NHTSA) defines an alcohol-related accident as one in which a driver or a nonoccupant (such as a pedestrian) had a blood-alcohol concentration of at least .01 grams per deciliter (g/dl) in a police-reported crash. The legal limit for a drunk-driving arrest is eight times that level: .08 g/dl. That can amount to as little as two or three drinks, depending on body mass and the amount of time in which the drinks are consumed.

- An **alcohol-related crash** kills someone **every 31 minutes** in the United States.

- Someone is injured in an **alcohol-related accident** every **2 minutes.** (NHTSA)[21]

The slowed reflexes of a driver under the influence of alcohol can lead to a deadly accident.

It does not take much alcohol to impair a driver's reflexes, and this is particularly true for young people. Teens generally weigh less than adults and are less aware of how their bodies and reflexes react to even one alcoholic drink.

The American Automobile Association (AAA) has estimated that after one or two drinks, a driver aged sixteen to nineteen is seven times more likely to be killed in a crash than a sober driver of any age.[22] Why is the risk so high?

Many young drivers who died in motor vehicle crashes had a blood-alcohol level below the legal limit. Even one drink may be one drink too many. [23]

Driving can be dangerous, even for a driver with sharp senses. Once alcohol reaches the brain, it slows the messages carried along the nerve fibers. Only a small amount of alcohol is required to decrease reaction time and create a relaxed feeling. Obviously, this is not the best way to perform a task that requires snap decisions and quick reflexes, such as driving.

This is why some states have adopted low- or zero-tolerance limits for drivers under age twenty-one. Violators lose their driver's licenses. These are also called "use and lose" laws.

3 2541 00006 288 0

A police officer may put suspected drunk drivers through several tests to determine their sobriety, including having them walk in a straight line.

TWENTY-ONE—THE MAGIC NUMBER?

At age eighteen, Americans can vote in elections, risk their lives in wars, and incur financial debt. However, they are still three years away from being able to drink an alcoholic beverage legally.

This was the argument used by many eighteen-, nineteen-, and twenty-year olds who opposed the National Minimum Drinking Age Act signed by President Ronald Reagan in 1984. The act gave states two years to pass age-twenty-one laws before federal highway money would be withheld. All fifty states complied, doing away with road trips to a nearby state where the drinking age was eighteen. In 1998, the NHTSA estimated that sixteen thousand lives had been saved as a result of the new age-twenty-one laws.

"Right now, you have a senior in college buying alcohol for his friends who are sophomores," says Dr. William DeJong, professor of social and behavioral sciences at the Boston University School of Public Health. "That's much better than having a senior in high school buying alcohol for his friends."[24] Such behavior used to be common prior to the age-twenty-one laws.

Some people point to other factors to explain the lower drunk-driving death rate. For example, are all those saved lives the result of just the age-twenty-one laws, or are safer roads and better law enforcement every bit as responsible?

Even many proponents of the higher drinking age admit that twenty-one is not a magic number. "I'm of the mind that twenty-one, though maybe not the perfect age, is an age that this country has basically gotten used to," DeJong says.[25]

Teens who would like to see the legal drinking age lowered do have some supporters in the academic and scientific worlds. One of their arguments is that the higher drinking age creates a "forbidden fruit" mentality: Teens eager to rebel against authority will do the very thing they are not allowed to do. College students, some argue, are going to drink anyway, and making it illegal creates unnecessary tension between students and law enforcement.

It's difficult, however, to argue with the evidence. In 1983, a year before the National Minimum Drinking Age Act was passed, 88 percent of high school seniors stated that they had consumed alcohol in the past year, and 41 percent admitted to binge drinking. By 1997, alcohol use by high school seniors had fallen to 75 percent, and the number of binge drinkers had dropped to 31 percent.[26]

Of course, there is no credible evidence that young people will learn to drink responsibly just because they are not allowed to start drinking until they're older. Nevertheless, concludes Jim Hall, chairman of the National Transportation Safety Board, "State age-twenty-one laws are one of the most effective public policies ever implemented in the nation."[27]

The decision to drive while under the influence of alcohol can ruin many lives.

EVERLASTING CONSEQUENCES

Still, a decrease in drunk-driving deaths will not bring back a single innocent victim. Seventeen-year-old Donn'elle McGraw died when a college student decided to get behind the wheel with some friends after drinking at the beach. Casey McCary Bloom was sentenced to twenty-one years in jail for his mistake. In an editorial he wrote for the University of Florida's student newspaper, Bloom urged others not to make the same mistake:

"No physical punishment I receive will compare to the emotional punishment I have been going through

and will go through for the rest of my life. There is not one person or family that should ever have to go through what the families of the victims and I have been through. It just isn't worth it. I ask that you please hear what I have written and understand the irreversible consequences of drinking and driving. I was a college student who thought this could never happen to me. Well, as you know, I was dead wrong. I had no intentions of ever hurting anyone. But because of the decision I made to get behind the wheel of a car, my life has been permanently affected. Don't make the mistake I did."[28]

After years of battling alcoholism, Lynne Boyer has returned to competitive surfing.

2 Youth Alcoholism

> "I thought I was too young to be an alcoholic. I was too smart to be an alcoholic. I was in denial."
>
> [—College student in Ohio]

ALCOHOLISM: IT'S NO GAME

Lynne Boyer was a surfing prodigy. Shortly after high school, she joined the fledgling world-surfing tour and began to master the waves. "I had dreams and visions of being like a tennis star, like Chrissie Evert and Martina Navratilova," she says. "It seemed like it was so easy. I loved it so much and it was a fun thing to do. That you could make money at it was like a bonus."[1]

Lynne quickly won two world championships, and her matches with fellow Hawaiian Margo Oberg were legendary. It seemed nothing could stop her—until alcohol brought her down as no wave ever could.

Many teens turn to rehabilitation programs when they find themselves in the grip of alcoholism.

Drinking became a part of Lynne's routine. She would stumble out of bars late, with only a few hours to sleep before her competitions. She would wake up with hangovers. And still, she would win. "I told myself that I couldn't be an alcoholic if I was winning contests."[2]

"It took me 13 years of being sober to make surfing fun again. . . . I finally learned that if you want something, you have to work for it. And it makes it even sweeter when you do."

—Lynne Boyer[3]

NO MORE DENIAL

The day arrived, however, when Lynne could no longer deny she had a problem. She was lethargic. She began taking drugs. She stopped surfing and became a drifter, picking up odd jobs. Alcoholism had a grip on her, and she had to find a way to break free.

Fortunately for Lynne, her family helped. They saw her through rehabilitation and self-help programs.

Lynne threw herself into a forgotten passion—art. She picked up competitive surfing again, too, enjoying it more than she ever had before.

Not everyone is as fortunate as Lynne. Alcoholism knocks countless Americans off far more than a surfboard. It bounces them from their jobs, their families, and their lives. Many never recover.

ALCOHOL ABUSE VERSUS ALCOHOLISM

Alcohol abuse, or "problem drinking," is the overuse of alcohol, often to the point of drunkenness.[4] You can abuse alcohol without being an alcoholic. And body mass is a key factor in how alcohol affects each person. There is no absolute standard.

Nearly **14 million Americans— 1 in every 13 adults**—abuse alcohol or are alcoholics.[5]

Symptoms of alcoholism include craving alcohol and the inability to stop drinking.

Alcoholism is an addictive dependency on alcohol characterized by craving (a strong need to drink), loss of control (the inability to stop drinking), physical dependence on alcohol, **withdrawal** symptoms if alcohol cannot be obtained, and alcohol tolerance (requiring increasing amounts of alcohol to become drunk).[6] It is recognized as a disease by the medical community.

KNOW THE PATTERNS

Although alcohol abuse does not always lead to alcoholism, drinkers who abuse alcohol over time are at risk for becoming alcohol dependent. Drinking when it is dangerous to do so (before driving, for example); drinking excessive amounts frequently; and having interpersonal, legal, or other problems that arise because of drinking are all signs of an alcohol-abuse pattern.

The NIAAA sets two drinks per day for men and one per day for women as the limits to safe drinking.[7] But sometimes even that amount is unsafe. For example, any drinking while driving, pregnant, or taking certain medications can be dangerous. For youths, the only safe limit is no drinking at all.

ALCOHOLISM OR ALCOHOL ABUSE?

Alcoholism differs from alcohol abuse in several ways. First, there is no known cure for alcoholism. An alcoholic who has not had a drink in several years—or even decades—can still suffer a **relapse**. All it takes is one sip. Alcoholism is chronic (always there), progressive, and potentially fatal.

The disease can be treated, and the symptoms can be reduced by avoiding alcohol. Detoxification, psychotherapy, group therapy, self-help programs, and nutritional therapy are some of the ways alcoholics can battle their disease.

Studies show that alcohol problems are highest among adults aged eighteen to twenty-nine. Understanding abuse patterns helps young people avoid problems associated with alcohol abuse.

Of youths aged 12–17 who say they drink heavily,

- **77%** had at least one serious problem related to drinking in the past year
- **20%** reported psychological problems related to their drinking
- **12%** reported related health problems.[8]

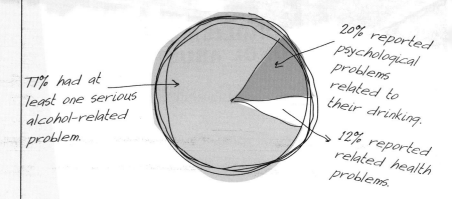

77% had at least one serious alcohol-related problem.

20% reported psychological problems related to their drinking.

12% reported related health problems.

PROBLEMS IN A BOTTLE

A variety of medical problems are associated with alcohol abuse. The human body was not made to withstand prolonged use of alcohol, particularly heavy drinking.

There are social consequences to alcohol abuse as well, particularly when that abuse starts young. Correlations between drinking and other teen problems—such as poor academic performance, delinquency, the use of other drugs, depression, and promiscuous sex—need to be explored.

Adolescents are going through physical and emotional changes, exploring new opportunities, and making significant choices—sometimes for the first time in their lives. It can be dangerous for such changes and choices to be blurred by the effects of alcohol.

Whether to drink alcohol or not is just one of many difficult choices that teens face.

Alcohol has been implicated in more than **40% of all academic problems in college.**[9]

ACADEMICS

It came as no surprise when, in 2003, American Medical Association (AMA) research showed that teenage drinkers, as a group, performed worse in school than their nondrinking peers. They scored lower on memory, vocabulary, and visual-spatial tests.[10] Scientists know that alcohol problems are consistently tied to lower grades, poor attendance, and increased dropout rates.

In the National Household Survey on Drug Abuse for 2000, heavy drinkers and binge drinkers were four to six times more likely than nondrinkers to report having skipped school or cut classes, and twice as likely as nondrinkers to say that their schoolwork is poor.[11]

Joe did not need statistics to tell him his drinking was causing problems in school. In an interview when he was eighteen, he said he had been an alcoholic for as long as he could remember. By sixth grade, his academic performance had declined considerably. His grades? "Just down the tubes," he says.[12]

"Lots of stuff was going through my head, and it wasn't school. Seventh grade was even worse. . . . I flunked every class—every single class I took all year. F, F, F, F." —Joe

Students who abuse alcohol are more likely to have problems in school.

DELINQUENCY

One reason Joe was able to get away with his drinking for so long was the fact that he was not considered a troublemaker. The same cannot be said for many teens who abuse alcohol.

In a recent NIAAA survey of eighth- and tenth-graders, alcohol use was significantly associated with both risky behavior and victimization (hurting others). This relationship was strongest among eighth-grade boys, but it was evident among the other groups as well.[13]

Within those other groups was Miranda, who realized she was an alcoholic by age sixteen.[14] Once a smiling, fun-loving girl who enjoyed life, she began to notice huge changes in her personality after drinking became a bigger part of her life in junior high and high school. The changes scared her.

Studies have shown that teens who abuse alcohol are more likely to get in fights.

Miranda started stealing from her family to support her drinking and marijuana use. "My moods were really crazy," she says. She found herself saying hurtful things to her friends, aware that it was wrong but unable to stop herself.

"It wasn't that I didn't remember what I said or anything. Your judgment gets so bad—at least mine did—that I knew I was doing wrong, but I didn't care." —Miranda[15]

Youth Alcoholism

In 2003, the National Survey on Drug Use and Health looked at youths aged twelve to seventeen to determine how alcohol use correlated with six specific delinquent behaviors. The results of the survey were telling.

The percentage of youths who engaged in the delinquent behaviors was highest for heavy drinkers. However, there was a correlation between all six behaviors and any alcohol use.[16]

THE SIX DELINQUENT BEHAVIORS:

- Getting into a **serious fight** at school or work

- Taking part in a **fight** in which a **group of friends** fought against another group

- **Attacking someone** with the intent of doing serious harm

- **Stealing or trying to steal** anything worth more than **$50**

- **Selling illegal drugs**

- Carrying a **handgun**

—2003 National Survey on Drug Use and Health

Parents who don't allow teenagers to drink alcohol at home can help their kids avoid serious substance abuse problems.

DRUG USE

Does teen alcohol abuse lead to drug use? Conversely, does teen drug use lead to alcohol abuse? Both can be true, and both alcohol and drugs are a problem for many youths.

CASA has concluded that children who begin drinking alcohol by age fifteen stand a 67 percent chance of progressing to other drugs. CASA also found that those who delay their first drink until age twenty-one are almost certain not to progress to other drugs.[17]

"Drug abuse is preventable. If boys and girls reach adulthood without using illegal drugs, alcohol, or tobacco, they probably will never develop a chemical dependency problem. Aggressive efforts to prevent underage use of tobacco and alcohol are essential to the prevention of illicit drug use."
—Barry McCaffrey, former Office of National Drug Policy director[18]

GATEWAY TO TROUBLE

Alcohol is sometimes called a gateway drug because it can be a first step toward the use of other drugs. The 1992 National Drug Control Strategy, issued by President George H. W. Bush, directly tackled the issue of alcohol abuse and made it an integral part of national drug-prevention policy. It still is. The strategy's policy statement confirms that a strong anti-alcohol campaign must be a key element in the fight against drugs.

One study found that teens who are allowed to drink at home are more likely to use alcohol and other drugs outside the home. They are also more likely to develop serious behavior and health problems related to substance abuse.[19]

DEPRESSION

There is the "chicken or egg" question about alcohol abuse and depression, too. One thing is certain: A strong relationship exists between depression and alcohol abuse, no matter which comes first.

A study of college freshmen found that students with anxiety disorder were twice as likely to be alcohol abusers than those without this disorder.[20] Another study found that college students who abused alcohol were almost four times as likely to have a major depressive disorder than other students.[21]

Alcohol abuse can increase feelings of depression and in some cases increase the likelihood of suicide attempts or other harmful behaviors.

SUICIDE

The link between alcohol abuse and suicide is frightening. Because alcohol impairs judgment and reduces inhibitions, it can make a suicide more likely. Alcohol has a depressive effect as well, making its use especially dangerous for a teen feeling a high level of stress and anxiety.

RISKY BEHAVIOR

Drunk driving and suicide are not the only fatal outcomes for alcohol abuse. Consider the case of Gary, who started stealing gin and vodka from his father when he was thirteen.[22] As a high school sophomore, he went to a school dance drunk and vomited on the floor. Despite missing classes because of drunkenness, he charmed his teachers into passing him.

Gary would often have unprotected sex after drinking, and he eventually tested positive for HIV (human immunodeficiency virus). He blamed the girl he was with, rather than himself, his alcohol addiction, or his frequent lapses in judgment.

Risky sexual behavior and alcohol abuse go hand in hand. Alcohol lowers inhibitions and reduces reasoning ability. This makes a person more vulnerable to coercive, or forced, sexual activity.

Adolescent drinkers with alcohol problems are more likely than other drinkers:

- to be **sexually active**
- to **begin sexual activity** at younger ages
- to have a **higher number of partners.**[23]

ONE TIME IS ENOUGH

Tragedy can result from a single episode of drinking. Drunk driving is the most obvious cause of tragedy. But a drinker doesn't need to get behind the wheel for drinking to kill.

Alcohol is considered a major risk factor for drowning. Drownings include boating mishaps, where both alcohol-using drivers and impaired passengers are at risk.

Alcohol can also contribute to injuries and fatalities involving fire. A smoker may be less cautious with a cigarette or match when under the influence. Drinking can also put a smoker at greater risk of falling asleep with a lit cigarette in hand. Studies of burn victims indicate that death rates are higher for patients with high blood-alcohol concentrations than for those with no measurable blood alcohol.[24]

"Half of all injuries could be avoided by not drinking when you are driving, boating, operating machinery, feeling angry, or using a firearm."
—Louis W. Sullivan, former U.S. secretary of Health and Human Services[25]

WARNING SIGNS

So how do you know if you or someone you know has an alcohol problem? There's no standardized test you can take to know for sure. But there are some questions to help determine whether a person is a problem drinker or may become one.

Stealing alcohol or drinking in secret can both be signs of a drinking problem.

The CAGE questions help serve as a guide. According to the NIAAA, answering yes to even one suggests a possible problem. Answering yes to two or more means it is highly likely that a problem exists. Anyone in this category should see a doctor or health care provider immediately.

Most teens with a drinking problem will not recognize it on their own or go to a friend or relative for help. They may say, "I can stop whenever I want to" or "I'm just doing it to have a good time."

The CAGE Questions

C Have you ever felt you should **cut down** on your drinking?

A Have people **annoyed** you by criticizing your drinking?

G Have you ever felt bad or **guilty** about your drinking?

E Have you ever had a drink first thing in the morning (sometimes called an **eye-opener**) to steady your nerves or get rid of a hangover?[26]

MORE WARNING SIGNS

The National Clearinghouse for Drug and Alcohol Information established guidelines for helping to determine whether a teenage friend might have a drinking problem. Be on the lookout for these behaviors:

- getting drunk on a regular basis
- lying about how much alcohol he or she is using
- believing that alcohol is necessary to have fun
- having frequent hangovers
- feeling run-down, depressed, or even suicidal
- having "blackouts"—forgetting what he or she did while drinking.[27]

One of the most difficult aspects of diagnosing youth alcohol problems is denial by parents. It's hard for a parent to face the fact that a child might have a drinking problem. It's even harder for a teen to come to that conclusion.

Dr. Claudia Black, an Arizona-based expert in the field of addiction recovery, recognizes this dilemma. She says, "When parents have a child in trouble, it's only normal that they would deny or minimize the extent of the problem. It's almost impossible to be objective when looking at our own children. Parents see grades drop, a negative change in friends, anger outbursts, and isolating behavior, and still [don't] see that there could be an alcohol or drug problem."[28]

GETTING CREATIVE TO CURB UNDERAGE DRINKING: ACT I

It is nearly impossible to keep track of all the horror stories involving teenage drinking—drunk-driving fatalities, alcohol-fueled violence, drinking binges that turn deadly.

Some teens hoping to prevent such tragedies in their towns are using their creative abilities to battle alcoholism—ideally, before it starts. They are turning to theater to portray topics that are sometimes difficult for children to discuss with their parents. Bringing drinking issues to life in this way can break the ice and make parents more aware of how prevalent alcohol might be in their children's peer groups.

"I think they don't know how often it is happening," says eighth-grader Kaitlyn Fraterman.[29] She belongs to a middle school leadership group in Brick, New Jersey, that put on a series of skits at a community forum on childhood drinking for parents.

Dan Woska, coordinator of the Brick program, said the skits portray how teens obtain alcohol and offer parents advice on how best to approach the subject with their children. The stories follow the paths of three friends from their earliest days of experimenting with alcohol into their college years.

"I heard peach schnapps is yummy," says a girl in one skit, exploring her parents' liquor cabinet and offering a bottle to her friends.

"Ooh, this stuff smells funny," responds another girl, who suggests they try mixing rum with Coke, because she heard it tastes good.

"It makes you feel good," adds a boy.[30]

The skits are not meant to win awards or become major motion pictures. They are meant to let parents know about some of the issues their children might be facing without their knowledge. They also provide cues about how to address those issues.

In Tucson, Arizona, a group called Clean and Sober Theatre (CAST) uses performances to tell the real-life stories of teens and young adults affected by alcohol and drugs. Seventeen-year-old Sara Meinecke joined CAST to get a handle on what she recognized as a growing problem in her life. She had been sober for three months when she was interviewed for a series on youth drinking. Her friend, seventeen-year-old Elise Lopez, said that CAST does much more than convey useful information to the audience. The group also provides positive support for CAST members who are battling addiction.

"There's always something there for you to get involved in—theater or art or sports," Lopez told the *Arizona Daily Star*. "I feel like a positive role model because of CAST."[31]

Many teens are faced with alcohol abuse in their homes.

3 Teen Alcoholism and the Family

"Kids don't read their parents' lips. They watch their parents' actions."

[—Joseph A. Califano Jr.[1]]

Almost one-quarter of American children live in a household where at least one parent or other adult is a binge drinker or a heavy drinker. So states a recent CASA study.[2]

SOMETHING TO PASS DOWN?

Having a parent who drinks heavily is troubling. Close relatives of alcoholics are two to four times more likely to have alcohol problems than people who are not related to an alcoholic.[3] Studies indicate that this increased risk cannot always be explained by their environment. Alcoholism can also have a genetic, or hereditary, aspect. A great way to examine the hereditary factors is to study twins.

Studying alcoholism among twins has provided strong evidence that some factors contributing to alcoholism are determined by genetics.

TWINS AND ADOPTEES

Identical twins, whose genes are exactly the same, show a strong bond when it comes to alcoholism. Of course, most twins are raised together, so it's almost impossible to remove the social factors from such studies. That's why a study of adopted children is so convincing.

The **identical twin** of an alcoholic may have up to a **60% greater risk** of becoming an alcoholic, too. A fraternal twin has about a **30% greater risk** of alcoholism.[4] This difference is evidence that alcoholism has a genetic element.

Adopted children of alcoholics who were raised in non-alcoholic households showed up to a fourfold increased risk for severe alcohol problems, even when they had no knowledge of their biological parent's alcoholism. Even if one of the adoptive parents was an alcoholic, the child faced no greater risk of alcoholism.[5]

A GENETIC LINK

In 2004, U.S. scientists demonstrated a link between a specific gene and the risk for alcohol dependence. Within a year, a similar study in Russia found more evidence that alcoholism has a strong hereditary component.[6]

"Alcoholism is a complex disease, and an individual's vulnerability is affected both by the set of genes they inherit, and the environments they are exposed to, including their behaviors," says Howard J. Edenberg, a professor of medical and molecular genetics at the Indiana University School of Medicine.[7]

SOCIAL INFLUENCES

Genetics plays a role in the risk for alcoholism, but social factors also shape drinking behaviors. In fact, even strong proponents of the hereditary basis will tell you that someone with a higher genetic risk for alcoholism is not doomed to a life of alcohol dependence.

Children of alcoholic parents may drink because they receive little love at home.

Parents who cannot control their drinking often spend more time drinking and with drinking's effects—drunkenness, hangovers, irritability, and so on—and less time nurturing their children.[8]

Parents who drink excessively often show more tolerance for teen drinking, as well. If they do not view their own heavy drinking as a problem, they are less likely to view their child's drinking as a problem.

Parents who preach the dangers of drinking yet engage in problem drinking themselves set a bad example. They also become less trustworthy because their actions don't match their words.

Higher levels of parental nurturing and warmth have been associated with lower levels of alcohol and substance abuse in children.

Parents who abuse alcohol often don't realize the long-term effects that their drinking can have on their children.

CODEPENDENTS

People who live with an alcoholic and are affected by that person's drinking are sometimes called co-alcoholics or **codependents**.[9] Codependents have a hard time with self-esteem, according to alcohol counselor Robert Subby. They may struggle to express feelings, have trouble making decisions, feel powerless, and constantly seek the approval of others. They may feel responsible for the behavior of their alcoholic family member.[10]

One way a child living in a codependent household might try to cope is by taking on the parent's household responsibilities, such as cooking or cleaning.

In her book *It Will Never Happen to Me*, Claudia Black notes that children in codependent families are particularly affected by the pain of growing up in such a setting. They cope by taking on one of these dysfunctional roles:

- The Responsible One tries to protect both the alcoholic and the family from the consequences of alcoholism. This child literally grows up too soon.
- The Adjuster adapts to the wild mood changes of alcoholism. This child might try to throw the drinker out of the house one minute and beg that person to stay the next minute.
- The Placater tries to minimize the conflicts in an alcoholic family, preferring to avoid outbursts instead of facing problems head-on.[11]

Black says that a child may also try to distract attention from problems at home by "acting out"—being a trouble-maker or a low achiever. Of course, children should not have to take on any of these roles. Each of the dysfunctional roles is likely to damage a young person's self-esteem at a time in life when building self-worth is of the utmost importance.

GROWING UP TOO SOON

From the time she was a toddler, Lani took care of the housework and fended for herself in the kitchen.[12] When she was in eighth grade, her alcoholic mother disappeared for three days after a party. Lani did not know who her father was, never attended the same school for more than a year, and frequently fed and took care of her mother. Lani's mother said she needed the booze to keep going.

"My mother was intelligent. I always thought she had great potential. The hardest thing I ever did was to let go of my hopes for her. She was just too sick to ever get better."

—Lani, on her alcoholic mother[13]

Even in families where alcohol abuse is a problem, providing stable daily activities, such as eating dinner together, can help prevent future problems with alcohol for children.

Lani adjusted to her nightmarish childhood by becoming "the responsible one," trying to protect herself and her mother from her mother's behavior. The problem was, no one could protect her mother from herself—particularly not a child. Lani leaned on her grandmother as much as possible and gained strength from her. But after her grandmother died, Lani had nowhere to turn.

So Lani began drinking, and by age sixteen she was a heavy alcohol abuser. Some days she could not remember where she had been—only that she had been drinking. One day, she looked in the mirror and was horrified. The face she saw resembled her mother's.

Lani decided right there and then to stop drinking. She honored her choice. Today she is married and trying to raise her own three children in a warm, caring environment—free of alcohol or substance abuse.[14]

THE ALCOHOLIC HOUSEHOLD

Lani worries that, because of her mother, she has a genetic predisposition to alcoholism. But she knows that a child's upbringing plays a big role, too.

Lani is on the right track. Parents who provide a nurturing experience at home—even in a home that includes an alcoholic—can help children avoid the pitfalls.

A 1979 study headed by S. J. Wolin showed that families with alcoholic members who kept stable behavior patterns for everyday activities—such as meals, special occasions, and family routines—had children with fewer alcohol problems. Preserving the family rituals, the authors note, provided more stability, predictability, and perceived support for those children.[15] Consistent and fair rules, positive emotional factors such as warmth and nurturance, and open communication were other factors that correlated with better-adjusted children who had fewer alcohol problems.[16]

"In the alcoholic's family, the broken promises are endless. . . . As long as there's abusive drinking, the liquor and not the family will be the number-one priority."

—Recovering alcoholic[17]

CHILDREN OF ALCOHOLICS:

- are at high risk for developing alcohol and other **drug problems**

- often **live with pervasive tension** and stress

- have **higher levels of anxiety** and depression

- may do **poorly in school**

- may experience **problems with coping**[18]

CHILDREN OF ALCOHOLICS

Government studies have found that children of drinking parents are less likely to see drinking as harmful and more likely to start drinking earlier. They are more likely to associate with kids who have tried alcohol at ages ten and eleven, increasing the probability for alcohol use and abuse by the child.[19]

Alcoholism is also associated with other family problems, such as child abuse and marital unhappiness. CASA found that alcohol- and drug-abusing parents are three times more likely to abuse their children and four times more likely to neglect them than sober parents.[20]

CHILD ABUSE

Each year, more than 1 million children are confirmed as victims of child abuse and neglect by state child protective service agencies.[21] The Children of Alcoholics Foundation reports that 40 percent of confirmed cases of child abuse and neglect involve the use of alcohol or other drugs.[22]

A parent's alcoholism can contribute to a stressful and sometimes dangerous environment for children.

Marital problems are often made worse by alcohol abuse, and the effects are often felt by children later in life.

These figures suggest that alcohol and substance abuse are involved in more than four hundred thousand cases of child abuse every year. Both alcoholism and child abuse carry a social stigma and, unfortunately, go largely unreported. We can only guess how those numbers would grow without denial and secrecy.

MARITAL PROBLEMS

Psychiatrist and addiction specialist Dr. Marc Alan Schuckit is the author of *Educating Yourself About Alcohol and Drugs: A People's Primer.* He began a long-term study of 453 sons of alcoholics. He also interviewed the wives of these sons. He found that women married to alcoholics drank more often and more heavily themselves and were more likely to be alcohol abusers.[23]

"People who drink a lot tend to congregate with other people who drink a lot," Schuckit says, "which tends to magnify the probability that drinking will lead to severe problems."[24]

In 2004, *Psychology Today* cited a study indicating that "adults who grew up with an alcoholic parent are a third more likely to end up divorced." It went on to note that, among one thousand college students, those with a parent or parents who were heavy drinkers held a far more negative view of marriage than those whose parents were light drinkers.[25]

BREAKING THE CYCLE

This does not mean that children of alcoholics must accept that they will become alcohol abusers, abuse their own children, or experience marital troubles. Yes, some sons and daughters, no matter how much they dislike their parents' drinking, will turn to alcohol as a way of handling problems. But others will break the cycle. One such person is Shirley Franklin, mayor of Atlanta, Georgia.

For a long time, Mayor Franklin kept quiet about her experience of growing up with an alcoholic father. Eugene Haywood Clarke Jr. had been a promising young lawyer with his own practice in Philadelphia and a supportive family—a wife, Ruth, and a young daughter who would go on to become the first woman elected mayor of Atlanta.

Ruth said her husband's decline began around the time someone else was nominated for a position Eugene had wanted. Eugene started coming home drunk from work, and clients began to complain. At age thirty, Eugene lost his license to practice law.

Franklin's parents eventually divorced as her father's life grew more and more unstable. She once saw him sleeping on a sidewalk and crossed the street to avoid him. After he showed up drunk at her high school orientation, she wrote "father, deceased" in the school directory.

"I just wanted to erase him from my life because it was too painful. I mean, how could someone with so much potential, how could someone who had done so well against so many odds not conquer this problem and make my life perfect?" —Mayor Shirley Franklin to the *Atlanta Journal-Constitution*[6]

TRIUMPH OVER TRAGEDY

With his daughter's help, Eugene Clarke did begin to put his life back together. At one point, illnesses nearly cost him his life. After this scare, he joined AA. His license to practice law was returned to him, and he was appointed as a judge. He shared a close relationship with his daughter until his death in 1998.

Mayor Franklin spoke openly about her father's alcoholism in a 2003 speech. Her father's life, she said, taught her that you can indeed start over.[27]

Atlanta Mayor Shirley Franklin (right) has spoken very openly about her and her mother's experiences with her father's alcoholism.

Pregnant women are advised not to drink alcohol because drinking during pregnancy can cause fetal alcohol syndrome.

SECRETS CAN HURT

Too often, family problems caused by alcoholism are "swept under the rug." Some people who have grown up in alcoholic homes suggest that the air of secrecy surrounding the problem can be worse than the problem itself.

"As difficult as it was dealing with my father's drinking, the greater pain for me was the secret-keeping. Adult children of alcoholics refer to the phenomenon as 'the elephant in the living room': You have a huge inescapable fact about your life that affects everything in your home, but nobody mentions it, although everybody's behavior is altered to accommodate or deal with it."
— Joyce Maynard in The Family Secret: Adult Children of Alcoholics Tell Their Stories[28]

FETAL ALCOHOL SYNDROME

Perhaps the most direct and severe way in which a parent's drinking can affect a child is **fetal alcohol syndrome** (FAS). This is a series of mental and physical birth defects that can develop in an unborn baby whose mother drinks alcohol during pregnancy.

The dangers of drinking during pregnancy had been suspected for some time, but it was not until 1968 that researchers in France formally defined FAS. FAS is now the top known cause of mental retardation in the United States.[29]

Babies with FAS face difficult lives. They are typically small or premature at birth, and their lag in physical and mental growth can be permanent.[30]

- **5,000–10,000 children are born with FAS** every year according to estimates, or 1 in every 500–1,000 live births.

- Women who are **chronic alcoholics** have a 2.5% chance of producing children with FAS.[31]

LIVING WITH FAS

Many children with FAS grow up to be alcoholics. That was the case with Sara.[32] She was born with abnormal facial features. Her body and head were always small for her age, and she had difficulty learning simple tasks. She carried these physical characteristics and learning troubles into adolescence and became socially removed from others her age. At sixteen, she began binge drinking, as her mother and father had done during her mother's pregnancy.

Fetal alcohol syndrome affects both the physical and mental growth of a child.

The link between the amount of alcohol consumed and the frequency and severity of FAS is not clear, but studies have shown that even one instance of binge drinking can damage a fetus.[33] The only absolutely safe quantity of alcohol a woman can consume while pregnant is none at all.

There is no known cure for FAS. There is treatment, as there is for any physical or mental disability. While options for people with disabilities have improved in recent years, many schools and workplaces still make few provisions for them.

AWARENESS

It was not that long ago that most people were ignorant of the dangers of drinking during pregnancy. Only since 1989 have alcoholic beverages had to carry a warning label about the risk of birth defects.

Fortunately, the risks are more widely known today, even among teens. In a survey published in 1995, 27,544 students were asked, "Can drinking alcohol while pregnant cause birth defects?" Of those, 81 percent answered "Yes, definitely." Another 16 percent answered, "Yes, probably," accounting for all but 3 percent of the survey group.[34]

Another danger is that a mother-to-be might not know she is pregnant at first. The CDC recommends that anyone who is sexually active and not using effective birth control abstain from using alcohol.[35] The results of not heeding such advice can be devastating.

Teen Alcoholism and the Family

YOUTH DRINKING IN THE HOME

Teens drink. Most of them will try alcohol. A large percentage will use it regularly. For millions, drinking will become a problem.

Resigning themselves to these facts, some parents take a different approach. Instead of teaching their children about the dangers of alcohol abuse and trying to keep them from drinking, some have decided that underage drinking in the home is better than having children experiment with alcohol away from their supervision.

In 2005, a fifteen-year-old in Tennessee died in a drunk-driving accident after a party where alcohol was served. The tragedy prompted Knox County district attorney Randy Nichols to say, "We're seeing more and more now that the parents are saying, 'Well this is kind of a rite of passage and if they're going to drink anyway, we'll let them drink here at home.' And we're trying to let parents know that even though it's at home, it's still illegal."[36]

Allowing teens to drink in the home is not only illegal, it is also dangerous. Several studies have shown that parents' permissive attitudes toward drinking correlate with a greater risk for drinking problems among youths.

Some parents are not so sure. In 2002, Gregg Anderson of West Warwick, Rhode Island, told his parents that he and his friends were planning to celebrate their senior prom with an all-night beer party at the beach. Gregg's parents offered an alternative. Concerned that some kids might drink and drive, they offered to host the party in their backyard.

About three dozen high schoolers showed up, and Mr. Anderson collected keys from every driver at the door. Heavy drinking ensued until 4:30 A.M. Police were called because of the noise. A few days later, Mr. Anderson was arrested for providing alcohol to minors. The charges were later dropped, but Anderson became known as the Prom Dad on talk-radio shows, and a debate stirred over whether he did the right thing.[37]

In 2005, *Time* magazine reported on an issue before the city council in Stratford, Connecticut. It was considering an ordinance that would allow police officers to enter a residence if they suspected that someone under twenty-one was consuming alcohol there, even if adults were present.[38]

At the time, 43 of the state's 169 municipalities had adopted the "house party ordinance." But Stratford was split over whether the measure would help curb underage drinking or simply threaten the privacy of its residents.

Psychologist and author Michael Thompson told the *Wall Street Journal* that parents who allow their children to drink "are sending a dangerous message that following the law is a matter of individual taste. I can't take issue with parents who let their own children drink at a family function, but those who allow other teens to drink in their homes are taking a huge risk."[39]

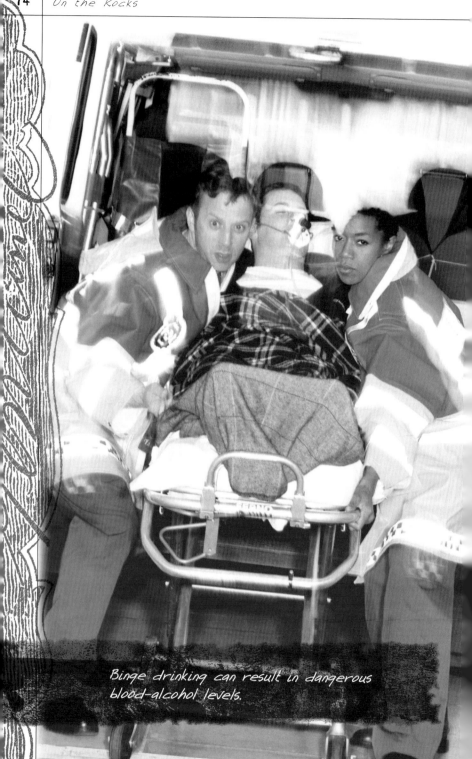

Binge drinking can result in dangerous blood-alcohol levels.

4 Binge Drinking

"We got a bottle of Bacardi 151 and, like, I was drinking it straight, completely straight. And I was pretty drunk. And that's the last thing I remember. I woke up at 6:30 A.M. the next morning in the emergency room, hooked up to IVs."

[—University of Maryland freshman Kelly Wells on *The News Hour with Jim Lehrer*[1]]

Believe it or not, Kelly Wells was one of the lucky ones. At least she woke up.

A fellow Maryland freshman, Danny Reardon, apparently drank himself unconscious at a party in 2002. He, too, had to be taken to a hospital by ambulance, but he never even saw the machines helping him cling to life. Danny suffered brain death after tests showed his blood-alcohol level had reached .5—more than six times the legal level of intoxication. He was nineteen.

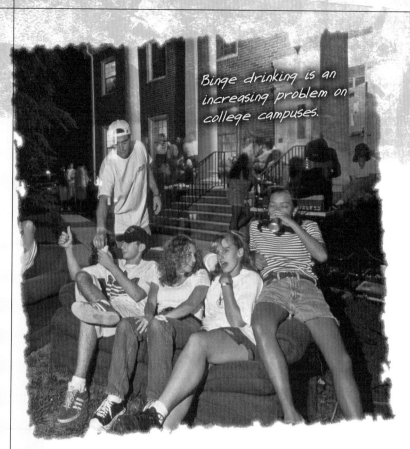

Binge drinking is an increasing problem on college campuses.

Danny's parents took him off life support after a week. "And no parent, as I did, should have to get up on a hospital gurney, and just hold his son and cry for hours that he's dead—never," said Danny's father, Daniel Reardon.[2]

Kelly and Danny had more in common than their school, their long nights of drinking, and their ambulance rides to the hospital. Both showed no signs of trouble in their adolescent lives. Danny was described by his father as a levelheaded teen with a sense of control—someone who knew his limits. Kelly said she was never a drinker in high school, but when she reached college she got into "the whole Thursday, Friday, Saturday 'let's get drunk'" routine.[3]

- In 2001, more than **1,700 college students aged 18–24 died from unintentional, alcohol-related injuries,** including motor vehicle crashes.[4]

- In 2001, **500,000 youths aged 18–24 were injured** under the influence of alcohol.[5]

- From 1998 to 2001, the number of **college students who drove under the influence** of alcohol jumped from **2.3** million to **2.8** million.[6]

WHAT IS BINGE DRINKING?

Binge drinking is a life-threatening problem that affects teens more than any other age group. It is most often defined as the consumption of five or more drinks in a row for males and four or more for females.[7] Its consequences can be deadly.

- More than **600,000 students aged 18–24 were assaulted** by another student who had been drinking in 2001.

- More than **70,000 students were victims of alcohol-related sexual assault** or date rape in 1998.

—Harvard School of Public Health study[8]

Many adults enjoy an alcoholic beverage or two over dinner, at a social event, or while watching a game. It is far less common for adolescents to engage in this kind of responsible drinking behavior. When kids drink, it is often with the sole purpose of getting drunk.

WHO ARE BINGE DRINKERS?

When the Harvard School of Public Health surveyed students at 116 U.S. colleges and universities in 1998, 42.7 percent of respondents had had a binge-drinking episode within two weeks of the survey. That was down slightly from the group's 1993 study.[9] Still, that large percentage should be a cause for concern to parents, professors, and law enforcement officials.

In 1996, binge drinking was reported by more than 30% of high school seniors, almost 25% of high school sophomores, and more than 15% of 8th-graders. (NIAAA)[10]

While binge drinkers can fit any description—just like alcoholics—this is one area where there are patterns. Binge drinking often starts the moment a student sets foot on a college campus, according to Joseph A. Califano Jr.: "Student binge drinkers tend to be younger—freshmen and sophomores, white, male—and tend to binge drink on weekends, which at many colleges begin on Thursdays."[11]

Much of the drinking that takes place on college campuses is binge drinking.

College students are often surrounded by a culture that promotes binge drinking.

A DANGEROUS AGE

Of course, both male and female students binge, and the behavior does not stop after those first two years. But binge drinking does appear to be a particular problem of teens and students. Lloyd Johnson, a University of Michigan researcher, contends that dangerous drinking begins to subside after age twenty-two.[12]

"You know, I thought my kids would get through this. I didn't think that one of them would pay for it with his life."

—Daniel Reardon[13]

High schools and colleges all over the country have tried every conceivable method of education, legislation, and enforcement in an attempt to cut down on binge drinking and the many problems that come with it. So why do students like Kelly Wells and Danny Reardon end up in emergency rooms or as the subject of heart-rending newspaper articles every school year? Many people are still searching for answers.

THE COLLEGE CONNECTION

You were not a big drinker in high school. Now you arrive on a college campus, living away from your parents for the first time in your life. Most of your high school friends are off at other schools, starting families, or delving into their first full-time jobs. You meet new friends, and the topic of conversation quickly turns to a quest: Where can we find a party? It's a scene that plays out every fall, and the partying continues through the school year.

Young people starting college are confronted with challenges: independence, more insecurity than perhaps they ever felt in the past, the need to conform or fit in. These are some of the reasons college students binge at a significantly higher rate than their noncollege counterparts.[14]

Binge drinkers rarely consider the dangerous effects their behavior could have on themselves or other people.

"In these college settings, where about one half of students are under age twenty-one, regular use and abuse of alcohol is part of many students' environments," says Dr. Henry Wechsler, lead author of the Harvard study.[15]

Wechsler and his colleagues surveyed about seven thousand underage college students and about five thousand students aged twenty-one to twenty-three about their drinking. The results?

- Most underage students reported that it was "easy" or "very easy" to obtain alcohol.
- Underage students were more likely to obtain alcohol inexpensively and to drink in private settings, such as in dorms and at parties.
- 63 percent of the underage students reported drinking in the past thirty days.
- 74 percent of the older students reported drinking in the past thirty days.

- 42 percent of the underage students said they had consumed five or more drinks at least once during the last thirty days.
- 27 percent of the older students said they had consumed five or more drinks at least once during the last thirty days.[16]

A CULTURE OF DRINKING

So why is underage drinking such an accepted part of the college experience? The American Council on Alcoholism says young students often turn to alcohol to relieve boredom and to connect with other students.[17] Alcohol decreases inhibitions.

Drinking has become an accepted part of college social life. According to William DeJong, alcohol may function as a psychological defense against feelings of helplessness. College students frequently experience such feelings. Drinking imitates adult behavior, DeJong notes, while at the same time signaling rebellion against authority. And it takes place in an environment where intoxication is valued by a large percentage of the population.[18]

"**Parents tend to see drinking** and occasional bingeing **as a rite of passage rather than a deadly round of Russian roulette.**" —CASA[19]

Shortly after the fall 1997 semester began at Louisiana State University (LSU), police found about two dozen young men unconscious on the floor of a fraternity house. Each had consumed the equivalent of twenty-four drinks. One of them, Benjamin Wynne, died with a blood-alcohol level of .588.[20] Weeks later, Massachusetts Institute of Technology (MIT) freshman Scott Krueger went to a frat party. He drank until his blood-alcohol level was five times the legal limit for a driver, fell into a coma, and never awakened.[21]

CHANGING THE CULTURE

After some high-profile campus tragedies in the late 1990s, reducing alcohol abuse among college students became a priority at schools across the country. Some colleges use Alcohol 101, an educational video game in which a virtual student goes to a frat party and has his blood-alcohol level monitored as he drinks.

Others have invested in AlcoholEdu, another computer-based educational tool. It focuses on alcohol's impact on the memory through a series of interactive graphics and quizzes. AlcoholEdu is mandatory for freshmen at several schools. Fraternities and sororities using AlcoholEdu saw a 14 percent decline in heavy drinking.[22]

EDUCATION WORKS

Education, it seems, has worked better to curb college binge drinking than the gruesome footage of drunk-driving accidents and alcohol-induced vomiting that some schools have

The enforcement of strict drunk driving laws helps save lives.

shown to incoming students. "There's absolutely no evidence those scare tactics worked," says DeJong.[23]

Some schools have tried to reverse the peer pressure that students face. In the late 1990s, a group of more than one hundred colleges followed the lead of Penn State president Graham Spanier. They used a national advertising campaign that included full-page ads in such major dailies as the *New York Times* and the *Boston Globe*.

The campaign didn't just inform students about the dangers of drinking. It tried to change ideas about drinking being desirable. Dartmouth College, for instance, covered its campus with flyers that professed, among other things, "Most Dartmouth students say that having alcohol at a party is not important to them."[24]

Whether these "social norms" programs are successful is not yet clear.[25] A Penn State woman celebrating her twenty-first birthday nearly died from downing twenty-one shots over two hours and raising her blood-alcohol level to an almost unheard-of .682. Penn president Spanier told the National Press Club, "Obviously, she and her friends didn't get the message."[26]

RULES AND ENFORCEMENT ON CAMPUS

Some schools ban alcohol entirely from their campuses. According to the U.S. Department of Health and Human Services, virtually every college campus in the country regulates alcohol in some manner.

LSU had banned alcohol at fraternities and campus events even before Benjamin Wynne's death. MIT announced stiffer penalties for underage drinking following the death of Scott Krueger. Violators under the new policy face penalties ranging from mandatory counseling to fines and expulsion.[27]

OTHER APPROACHES

Other colleges have taken different approaches to the problem of binge drinking. They set up "safe drinking harbors" on campus. For example, in the 1990s, Salisbury State University in Maryland converted a campus dining hall into a bar. The idea was to control the drinking of students twenty-one and older and keep them from driving while drunk.

- **Beer is banned** on 25% of U.S. college campuses.

- **Hard liquor is banned** on 33% of U.S. college campuses.

—U.S. Department of Health and Human Services[28]

"I favor campus pubs, if they are strictly enforced," DeJong says. "Even students under twenty-one enjoy them. There is food and entertainment. Nothing is accomplished by pushing alcohol entirely off campus."[29]

Harvard's Wechsler disagrees: "If you let them drink on campus, it doesn't mean that they'll only drink on campus." He has urged universities to take firm stands against underage drinking, binge drinking, and alcohol-fueled fraternity and sorority parties. He is backed by a *U.S. News and World Report* survey of more than a thousand college presidents. The survey found that schools that allow drinking on campus are three times more likely to have high percentages of binge drinkers.[30]

Many colleges and universities have tried to implement on-campus bars and pubs to promote legal and responsible drinking.

Dorm rooms provide privacy to many underage binge drinkers.

SKIRTING THE RULES

Even at campuses that rigorously enforce a strong alcohol policy, students find ways to skirt the rules. For most of the University of Notre Dame's history, a student could be expelled for being caught with alcohol on campus. The rules were relaxed in the 1970s, tightened again in 1978, and then altered to comply with Indiana state law. That is, students under twenty-one who are drinking are doing so illegally, on campus or otherwise.

The privacy of dorm rooms, however, has been generally respected. Students too young to drink at Notre Dame's Senior Bar have been able to drink in dorm rooms for years, as long as their noise is not disruptive.

NEW STANDARDS

Beginning in the early 1980s, Notre Dame allowed in-dorm dances with free-flowing alcohol once or twice a year. But in 2002, when the school saw that the drinking had become primary and the dances secondary, it announced that the dorms would no longer host such events.

Many students were outraged. One dorm president predicted: "This place will no longer be fun in ten years. I say that not as a warning but as a statement of the truth."[31]

The adult supervisor of one dorm expressed quite a different view in a school newspaper column. The truth, he said, is that even one of the nation's preeminent Catholic universities—one that places great emphasis on its substance-abuse and student-conduct policies and is a far cry from a "party school"—is not immune to the binge-drinking problem.

> **"Men and women have left Keenan Hall strapped to stretchers** with blood alcohol levels so high that they could not be awakened for six hours. One resident retched so violently that he tore his stomach. Sadly, this reality is **not particularly bad by campus standards."**
>
> —Notre Dame's Father Gary Chamberland[32]

A BROAD-BASED APPROACH

A 2002 NIAAA report outlines why many efforts to curb binge drinking by college students fail. Patterns of college drinking are so ingrained, the report says, that only broad efforts to alter the culture and social norms, both on campuses and in surrounding communities, are likely to succeed.

Says University of Rhode Island president and task force member Robert L. Carothers: "You have to first admit that you have the problem. Most colleges and universities don't really want to do that. Their efforts to deal with the problem are pretty half-hearted."[33]

The Harvard study found that, while fewer students drink at colleges that ban alcohol, those who do drink engage in just as much extreme drinking as students at colleges where drinking is permitted.[34] And student drinkers at schools where alcohol is prohibited experience alcohol-related problems at the same rate as their counterparts at schools where drinking is not banned.[35]

Binge drinking is not confined to college students—not by a long shot. Alcohol has been banned in some stadiums, both in North America and overseas, because of rowdiness, violence, and even deaths attributed to heavy drinking at concerts and sporting events.

"There is an environment out there of cheap alcohol sold at high volume—which is the fuel for binge drinking."

—Dr. Henry Wechsler[36]

Binge drinking while watching sporting events sometimes leads to rowdy or even violent behavior.

ALCOHOL: TOO POPULAR AS A PROM DATE

College is not the only place where binge drinking holds a certain level of acceptance. For many teens, high school prom night is not just the biggest dance of their junior or senior year. It is also a time to cross boundaries when it comes to high-risk behavior, including alcohol use and sexual activity. Drinking on prom night has become so widespread that many parents see it as a rite of passage—a necessary ritual for passing from childhood to adulthood.

If it is a rite of passage, it is often a fatal one. In 2005, the Chrysler Group's Road Ready Teens program and Mothers Against Drunk Driving (MADD) took a survey of teen drinking and driving. They found that 45 percent of teens feel pressure to drink and drive or to ride with someone who has been drinking on prom or graduation nights.[37] That pressure can force a high school student to make a choice, quite literally, between life and death. More than half of all fatal crashes on prom and graduation nights involve alcohol, according to the NHTSA.[38]

Kids also often see prom night as an excuse for binge drinking. And binge drinking is especially dangerous for teens, who are likely unaware of how large quantities of alcohol affect their bodies and their judgment.

Some high schools conduct breath tests before allowing students into their proms. A student who has been drinking is not admitted. Westfield High

School in Indiana is one such school, and Principal Rick Russ says the policy has been successful since it began in 2003.

A survey by Joseph McKinney, chairman of Ball State University's Department of Educational Leadership, found that 94 percent of principals thought that breath tests were effective in "discouraging drug and alcohol use among students."[39] But some students say they aren't. They say that the brunt of prom-night drinking takes place after the prom, at parties away from the school.

Other schools have taken different approaches. A Baltimore high school placed a totaled car in front of its campus before the prom, with a warning about prom-night drinking. Several schools offer post-prom alternatives to the drinking parties that many teens favor.

And then there is the tiny community of Silver Grove, Kentucky. It conducted a Grim Reaper Day in 1999 in reaction to a prom-night drunk-driving death the previous year. A student dressed as the Grim Reaper (a black-clad symbol of death) went from classroom to classroom choosing students to represent drunk-driving fatalities. At day's end, a school assembly was held at which a police officer, an emergency room nurse, and a judge discussed the consequences of drinking and driving. A 50 percent decrease in alcohol-related driving accidents among Silver Grove youth was charted the next year, enough to have officials call the event a big success.[40]

Even though the legal drinking age in Europe is lower than in the United States, there is less of a problem with binge drinking in many European countries than there is in the United States.

5   Youth Drinking and Society

"They were very intolerant of their peers who became intoxicated. It's a very easy way to get excluded from a group. . . . They think it's stupid, unacceptable, and that's true throughout most of Europe."

[—Dr. David J. Hanson, on attitudes toward drinking in Italy[1]]

Many of the problems connected to alcoholism and teens in the United States are not as prevalent in Europe, according to Dr. David J. Hanson. Italian, Greek, Spanish, and Portuguese cultures are among those in which moderate alcohol use is introduced at an early age. Hanson, of the State University of New York, argues that there are three keys to the successful use of alcohol in these cultures:

1. Viewing alcohol neutrally, as neither poison nor magical elixir.
2. Providing two acceptable options for alcohol use—abstinence and moderation—while not condoning or permitting abuse.
3. Learning about alcohol from an early age at home, in a safe, caring, and loving environment.

In these successful societies, abstainers and moderate drinkers respectfully coexist, with neither trying to force its views on the other. It's better, Hanson contends, "to learn about drinking in a parent's house than in a fraternity house—where too many young people now 'learn' about drinking, and learn badly."[2]

If you're twenty-one, responsible drinking can include having a glass of wine at dinner.

There is no question that European cultures are less restrictive when it comes to teen drinking. Eighteen-year-olds have legal access to alcohol in all European countries, although only wine or beer in some places. Some countries have no minimum drinking age. Others, including Italy, Greece, France, Spain, and Germany, have allowed drinking at age sixteen.[3]

Drunk-driving laws in those countries are strict, however, and many locals frown on drunkenness. This contrasts greatly with the United States, where intoxication is actually celebrated in some settings, such as college campuses.

A HEALTHY ATTITUDE

A 2005 *Chicago Tribune* article tells the story of Amy Jones, a Cal State Fullerton student who was twenty when she went to Europe to study for eight months. She researched drinking ages before she left and landed an internship writing for PubClub.com, a nightlife guide, while she was there. Amy documented her experiences as she and her friends enjoyed the nightlife in several European countries.

Hanson, who has studied teens and alcohol for thirty-five years, says that the "glass of wine with dinner" attitude separates many European cultures from the United States. "They just historically have had a much healthier, more accepting attitude toward drinking," he says of the European countries. "But they are rather intolerant of alcohol abuse."[4]

While drinking is an important part of many European cultures, problem drinking is less common.

"**Being twenty,** I was in a great position because I could go out and do all that stuff with my friends **. . . not necessarily get drunk, but have a glass of wine with dinner.**"

—Amy Jones in the *Chicago Tribune*[5]

"WET" AND "DRY" CULTURES

Cultures in which alcohol tends to be seen as evil by some—and in which groups have tried to contain or put a stop to drinking—are sometimes referred to as "temperance," "dry," "Nordic," or "ambivalent" drinking cultures. The United States is an obvious example.

Those in which more positive beliefs about alcohol are widespread are called "nontemperance," "wet," "Mediterranean," or "integrated" drinking cultures. Many European countries fall into this category. In general, drinking is not as big an issue in these countries.

A 1998 report from England's Oxford University found that nontemperance cultures had significantly fewer social problems related to alcohol than temperance cultures.[6] It also found that in wet cultures, such as many in South America, drinking behaviors were largely peaceful and harmonious compared with dry cultures.[7]

- **In Japan,** alcohol consumption has nearly **doubled over the last 30 years.**

- **In Russia,** it has been estimated that **40% of men and 17% of women are alcoholics.**[8]

Researchers continue to try to find solutions to the binge drinking problem in the United States.

Hanson has outlined several steps that might help countries such as the United States, where binge drinking has caused major problems. Among those steps are:

- Present moderate drinking and abstinence as equally acceptable choices.
- Make systematic efforts to identify and promote the distinction between acceptable and unacceptable drinking.
- Penalize unacceptable drinking firmly, both legally and socially.
- End the "demonization" of alcohol.[9]

"**I find it so funny.** On a Friday night you walk in downtown Windsor and **I'd say 85 percent of the people there are 19- or 20-year-old Americans who can't drink legally in the States.**"

—Canadian Orville Smith in the *State News*[10]

CLOSER TO HOME

You don't need to cross an ocean to observe cultural differences in teen alcohol use. The *State News* in East Lansing, Michigan, published a series of articles in 1998. The authors followed Michigan State University (MSU) students to a bar in Windsor, Canada, where nineteen- and twenty-year-olds could drink legally. Often a majority of the bar's patrons were underage American college students.

The series also compared the University of Windsor's record of alcohol-related offenses to Michigan State's during the period. It determined that, for every 1 such offense at the Canadian school, 130 were handled by MSU's Office of Judicial Affairs. Yet MSU's student population was only four times greater than Windsor's.[11]

Of course, this was hardly a scientific survey. But the

"*In communities in which early socialization to drinking is the norm . . . youngsters learn simultaneously how to drink moderately, how and why to avoid drunkenness, that drinking will not magically improve one's personality, and that excessive drinking illustrates weakness.*"

—*Professor Dwight B. Heath*[12]

prevalence of underage American drinkers across the border was so high—and the perception of American drinking habits so poor among the Canadians interviewed for the story—that a change in U.S. attitudes toward drinking seems worth considering.

Professor Dwight B. Heath is the author of *Drinking Occasions: Comparative Perspectives on Alcohol and Culture.* He writes that, in countries where drinking does not carry a "forbidden fruit" appeal for minors, healthier attitudes and behaviors tend to follow.

Of course, changing long-held attitudes is no easy task. It may be impossible.

A 1996 study of children ages nine to eleven found that children were **more familiar with Budweiser's television frogs** than Kellogg's Tony the Tiger, the Mighty Morphin' Power Rangers, or Smokey the Bear.

—Center on Alcohol Marketing and Youth[13]

ADVERTISING ALCOHOL

Parents remain the biggest influence on children when it comes to attitudes about alcohol. Views of drinking in the home shape the values and beliefs children take with them outside the home. But in a society in which television, newspapers, movies, and the Internet play a prominent role in popular culture, the messages teens get from it can also shape their attitudes.

There is evidence not only that alcohol ads have reached youngsters unintentionally while advertising to adults, but that some of these ads have specifically targeted minors. A 1997–2001 study on alcohol advertising in magazines found that the number of beer and distilled **spirits** ads tended to increase with a magazine's youth readership. For every 1 million underage readers (twelve to nineteen), researchers generally found 1.6 times more beer ads and 1.3 times more ads for distilled spirits.[14]

Teens are often exposed to alcohol advertising in magazines and other media.

Alcohol advertising is prominent at sporting events, such as car races.

TARGETING KIDS

The Center for Media Education found evidence of alcohol ads targeting youth on the Internet. In monitoring seventy-seven alcohol-promotion Web sites for two months in 1998, it found that 62 percent of those sites used marketing techniques that appealed to youth.[15]

The alcohol industry seems to make the strongest connections with children in TV ads.

In 1999, the Federal Trade Commission (FTC) called on advertisers to follow "best practice" policies, including not airing alcohol ads on TV programs and in other media with large underage audiences. Beer ads, however, are a staple of the Super Bowl, which as many as 40 percent of U.S. children watch every year.[16]

SETTING LIMITS

According to some estimates, alcohol companies spend more than 1 billion dollars annually on advertising. The FTC has tried to prevent advertisers from targeting children while allowing them to market their products to of-age consumers. It's a difficult balance.

Some people in favor of widespread alcohol advertising argue that there is no solid evidence to support claims that such ads make children more likely to drink. They say that companies are not trying to increase the number of drinkers but, rather, to convince a larger percentage of people who already drink to purchase their product.

DO ADS HAVE AN IMPACT?

Advertisers would not spend millions to spread the word about their products if they were not convinced such publicity would help them sell. Certainly, alcohol ads make their mark with the public. People associate Clydesdale horses with Budweiser and the "tastes great, less filling" ads with Miller Lite.

Whether those associations steer children toward drinking is harder to know. A *USA Today* survey in 1997 found that teens said alcohol ads have more of an impact on their decision about whether or not to drink than on their choice of a particular brand.[17]

Dr. Joel W. Grube, associate director of the Prevention Research Center of the Pacific Institute for Research and Evaluation, headed a study of the ways that children and adolescents interpret and respond to the images in alcohol ads. He determined that ads with music, animals, popular actors, humor, and story lines were generally well liked by youths aged nine to sixteen. The study verified that they are exposed to, like, and are aware of alcohol ads.[18]

Grube's study outlined several ways in which the effects of alcohol advertising on youths can be reduced. Among them:

- Reduce the exposure of children to alcohol ads by restricting the ads' time and placement. For example, limit alcohol sponsorships at youth sports events.
- Increase the media literacy and skills of young people. That is, help them understand the persuasive appeal of ads so that they can better distinguish perception from reality.
- Increase counteradvertising, or public-service announcements designed to discourage underage drinking and explain the dangers of alcohol abuse.[19]

IT WASN'T ALL HIS FAULT.

ADDICTION IS PHYSICAL. THE TREATMENT IS MEDICAL.

PR⚫META
overcomeaddiction.com

Chris Farley

REGENCY

This example of counteradvertising features actor Chris Farley who died at the age of 33 from the effects of alcohol and drug abuse.

COUNTERADVERTISING

"Drink responsibly." "We'll wait for your business." These are just two of the many counteradvertisements and slogans the alcohol industry has put out.

Anheuser-Busch announced in 2004 that it had spent more than $500 million since 1982 on responsible-drinking efforts. One 2005 ad campaign featured rap star Nelly, who reminded parents, "Your kids are your biggest fans, so talk with them about underage drinking."

RESULTS

Whether these public service announcements—or warning labels on bottles and cans—are effective is a matter of debate. The research is inconclusive.

And what about public service announcements telling young people to wait until they turn twenty-one to drink? While these ads have increased in recent years, underage drinking statistics in the United States have remained relatively constant.

In other words, these efforts are a step in the right direction but not nearly enough to make a substantial impact.

ALCOHOL IS EVERYWHERE

It's not just ads promoting alcohol as the key to a good time. It's TV shows too, along with music and many other forms of entertainment. Two of the most popular country music hits of 2005 were Brad Paisley's "Alcohol" and Kenny Chesney's "Keg in the Closet."

From the 1980s hit TV series *Cheers*, which was set in a neighborhood tavern, to the more contemporary *Two and a Half Men*, in which one of the main characters chugs booze while lifting weights—drinking appears to be a hit with American TV viewers. Again, research into the effects of such shows varies widely.

In one study,

- each extra hour per week spent **watching music videos increased the risk** of starting to drink by **31%**

- each extra hour per week spent **watching general TV programming increased the risk** by **9%.**[20]

In 1998, Stanford University researchers studied 1,533 ninth-graders at six San Jose, California, high schools. Their results indicate that a bombardment of scenes featuring alcohol use in music videos and other TV programming may help entice teens into trying their first drink.[21]

The authors of the study suggest that at least part of this increased risk is related to how alcohol use is portrayed on TV: "Alcohol use is portrayed more frequently by more attractive, successful, and influential people in a positive social context, often associated with sexually suggestive content, recreation, or motor vehicle use. In contrast, alcohol use is rarely portrayed in an unattractive manner or . . . associated with negative consequences."[22]

NASCAR DROPS THE GREEN FLAG ON LIQUOR SPONSORSHIPS

Everyone knows that drinking and driving don't mix. Everyone, it seems, but NASCAR.

NASCAR is the National Association for Stock Car Auto Racing. Drivers in the wildly popular and fast-growing sport were already zipping around tracks in cars with Budweiser, Miller Lite, and Coors Light paint jobs. Then in 2004, NASCAR opened its doors to hard liquor sponsorships, which were previously banned.

It was a move met by opposition. The AMA was concerned that lifting the ban would send a bad message about drinking and driving. In addition, "Our children need less exposure to alcohol, not more," said AMA president-elect Dr. J. Edward Hill.[23]

NASCAR had restricted advertising for hard liquor companies since the sport's "modern era" began in 1972, while allowing beer and malt liquor sponsorships. One of NASCAR's three major racing series is even called the Busch Series, after beer maker Anheuser-Busch. In lifting the hard liquor ban, NASCAR required companies to promote responsible drinking. "They appear to be trying to do it right," John Moulden, president of the National Commission Against Drunk Driving, told the Associated Press.[24]

This was hardly the first time the issue of hard liquor advertising met the public eye. Liquor companies had voluntarily agreed in 1948 not to advertise their products on TV. But in 1996, a Seagram's whiskey ad aired on a cable network, causing a public furor. Investigations were launched by the FTC and the Federal Communications Commission (FCC), and activists united in an effort to keep such ads off the air.

The FTC and FCC investigations made the major networks wary. Since then, however, several cable channels and local networks have relaxed their policies. It is no longer unusual to see cable TV ads for liquor brands.

In December 2001, NBC relaxed its fifty-year, self-imposed ban on liquor ads by airing spots from Smirnoff vodka that promoted responsible drinking. The network decided three months later not to run the next phase of Smirnoff's planned ad campaign, which marketed the product more directly.[25]

Today's TV industry, loaded with popular cable shows, has given the hard liquor companies an ad platform. Said Edgar Bronfman Jr., former chief executive of Seagram: "Someone had to take leadership and say, 'This is wrong.' There was this misperception that the alcohol in beer is somehow different from the alcohol in wine, which is somehow different than the alcohol in spirits. It's not."[26]

So, these days, you'll see all kinds of liquor ads circling the track.

Bill Wilson struggled with alcoholism for years before cofounding Alcoholics Anonymous.

6 | Calls for Help

"My name is Bill W., and I'm an alcoholic."

[—Bill Wilson, who cofounded Alcoholics Anonymous in 1935]

For twenty-first-century alcoholics, good help is easy to find. That was not the case when Bill Wilson was growing up in Vermont. His mother moved to Boston and his hard-drinking father to Canada, leaving Bill to be raised by his grandparents.

In his career, first as a soldier and later as a businessman, Wilson experienced a great deal of depression. He drank to help ease the pain. When his Wall Street investments did well, he drank to celebrate. When the stock market crashed in 1929, he drank to forget his losses. By 1933, Wilson and his wife were living with her parents, and by the following year he had been hospitalized four times.

Anyone who suffers with alcohol-related problems is welcome to attend their local AA meeting.

BIRTH OF A SOLUTION: AA

After a failed round of treatment for his alcoholism, Wilson became convinced that he could save himself by helping another alcoholic. He met with Ohio surgeon Dr. Bob Smith, another alcoholic, and the two decided that their own suffering could spur a method for helping themselves and others.

Smith died in 1950 and Wilson in 1971. Their legacy, however, lives on every time someone at an Alcoholics Anonymous (AA) meeting says, "I'm [name] and I'm an alcoholic." AA counts more than 2 million members in 150 countries.

THE TWELVE STEPS

At the core of AA is a twelve-step program laid out by Wilson in a book first called *The Way Out*, then *The Empty Glass*, and finally *Alcoholics Anonymous*. It is known as the Big Book, and millions of people over the years have credited the program's twelve "steps and traditions" with helping them to live sober lives. You can find the twelve steps at AA's Web site (www.alcoholicsanonymous.org).

There are no dues required to be a member of AA, and people who go to meetings are not required to speak. They can just sit and listen, and know that they are not alone in their troubles. Those who do speak usually give only their first name. Confidentiality is a core value of the group.

There is a spiritual element to the Big Book and references to God in the twelve steps. Wilson stressed, however, that members did not have to profess any religious beliefs.

PLACES FOR TEENS TO TURN

Problem drinkers of all ages are welcome at AA meetings. In fact, the AA Web site offers a simple online quiz for teens to help them determine whether they might have a drinking problem. It notes that the only requirement for membership is the desire to stop drinking.

Some groups are designed specifically to help teens, whose alcohol-related problems can differ widely from those of adults. One of the most prominent is **Alateen**. This is a program for teens with friends or relatives whose drinking problems are affecting their lives.

Alateen is a branch of **Al-Anon**, an organization founded in 1951 by the wives of two AA members. Using many of the basic principles that have worked in AA, Al-Anon teaches people that in order to help a drinker with his or her problem, they first have to help themselves.[1]

In 1956, a seventeen-year-old boy with one parent in AA and the other in Al-Anon founded Alateen. He recognized that, compared with adults, teens with an alcoholic family member often have to deal with different issues and concerns.

Al-Anon and Alateen meetings are not directed by professional counselors, but by the members themselves. These groups do not try to take the place of professional counselors. In fact, they recommend including counseling in a treatment program.

"If you try Alateen and you don't like it, it's only one meeting, and it doesn't cost anything," offers sixteen-year-old Jennifer, whose father is a recovering alcoholic. "If you

- **Al-Anon and Alateen have 26,000 groups** in 115 countries.
- In 2003, **Alateen members each had an average of 4 alcoholics in their lives.**[2]

want to, you can just sit back and listen. For me it was good because I didn't think I could talk to any of my friends."[3]

Some groups help alcoholics; others help their families. Still others focus on trying to stop the dangerous behaviors that problem drinking can provoke.

"It was good to hear that other kids had the same problems I did. You realize you're not alone out there. You don't feel as weird."

— Jennifer[4]

Treatment for alcohol addiction will often include group therapy.

MADD

Mothers Against Drunk Driving (MADD) celebrated its twenty-fifth anniversary in 2005. The well-known organization's roots grew out of tragedy. In 1979, a repeat-offending drunk driver hit a car driven by Maryland's Cindi Lamb head-on at well over 100 miles (161 kilometers) per hour. The collision made Lamb's daughter, five-month-old Laura, one of the world's youngest quadriplegics.[5]

Less than a year later, across the country, another repeat offender's drunk driving killed thirteen-year-old Cari Lightner. The man had been released on bail just days earlier on a hit-and-run drunk-driving charge, and he had two previous drunk-driving convictions. Yet he was carrying a valid California driver's license.[6]

In 1980, Cindi Lamb and Cari's mother, Candace Lightner, channeled their outrage into the formation of MADD. The organization spreads the word about the dangers of drunk driving and fights for stricter laws and better enforcement. MADD claims more than 3 million members and supporters in all fifty states, and it cites figures that show a 43 percent decline in alcohol-related traffic fatalities since the group's inception.[7]

SADD

In 1981, as MADD was being formed, two Wayland, Massachusetts, hockey players were killed in separate car crashes. Teacher Robert Anastas and his Wayland High School students decided to form a group to help young people avoid the risks of drinking and driving. They called it Students Against Driving Drunk (SADD). At its core is the Contract for Life, a two-way pact to be agreed upon and signed by the young person and a caring adult (usually, but not necessarily, a parent or parents). You can read the contract on SADD's Web site (www.sadd.org).

National chapters of SADD began forming in 1982. After the Contract for Life appeared nationally in newspaper advice columns in 1984, SADD's small headquarters office received almost fifty thousand requests for copies of the contract in just six weeks.[8]

Members of MADD try to raise awareness of the dangers of mixing alcohol and driving.

A high school student looks at her reflection in a mirror placed in the bottom of a coffin at a school assembly sponsored by SADD.

A NEW NAME

In 1997, SADD broadened its scope and changed its name, but the well-known initials stayed. Students stated that the same positive peer pressure, role models, and other strategies that helped them avoid drinking and driving could also help them with other dangerous behaviors, such as smoking, drug use, violence, and sexual promiscuity. SADD now stands for Students Against Destructive Decisions.

SADD's newsletters, research, conferences, Student Leadership Council, Student of the Year program, and, of course, the Contract for Life have drawn attention to the concerns of students nationwide. They also have helped teens and parents develop positive strategies for handling those concerns.

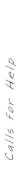

DO HELP GROUPS REALLY HELP?

AA, Al-Anon, Alateen, MADD, SADD, and other such programs offer help and support to people dealing with alcoholism and its effects. In addition to these groups, school counselors, teachers, doctors, professional counselors, and, of course, family members and friends, give teens struggling with alcohol issues countless places to turn.

Not everyone is convinced that programs like AA are the answer. Some research shows a high likelihood of relapse after joining. AA has also been knocked as a "one-size-fits-all" program for a problem that rarely follows a set pattern. Some have even suggested that AA can actually harm alcoholics by convincing them that alcoholism is for life, thus taking away their sense of control.

For teens, the trouble with help groups can be more practical. Introduce a young alcoholic to the twelve-step program, and the reaction is not always positive. "Some think it's a joke," says one teen.[9] He did at first, too. He chose sponsors who were most like him—kids who seemed cool. He never bothered to call them, then blamed them for his lack of progress. Finally, he asked someone else to pick his sponsor. He wound up with "a real straight dude, someone I never would have picked," and he worked his way through the twelve steps.

Certainly, not every program is for everyone. For some, AA is a lifesaver. For others, full-time counseling works better. Still others rely on their own resolve—truly putting the "self" in self-help.

"**If you want recovery,** try it our way. You won't be consumed any longer, and nothing hangs over you like the courts, guilt, and shame."

—A teenage AA member [10]

A WORLDWIDE IMPACT

There is no denying the importance of programs such as AA and Alateen, however. One of the most ambitious studies of AA's impact was undertaken by an international group of researchers in the 1990s. The study, which was directed by Klaus Makela and supported by the World Health Organization, found AA to be "the prototype of a new kind of social movement" with an international impact. [11]

The researchers were impressed that AA crossed political, cultural, and social boundaries. AA shows, they say, "that a system of thought and program of action developed in middle-class North America in the 1930s can be adapted and made relevant, while still maintaining its core features, in cultural environments as diverse as the slums of Mexico City, the factory towns of Poland, and the agricultural villages of Switzerland." [12]

There are many places where teens with alcohol-related problems can turn. People want to help, and many of them have faced and learned to overcome similar trials. Connecting with just one of those people can be the first step toward a life free from the bondage of alcoholism and alcohol abuse.

Many teens who struggle with the tough decisions surrounding alcohol find it helpful to share their feelings, and experiences with a group of their peers.

"I got sick and tired of being sick and tired. I didn't want that feeling anymore. . . . I had to make a decision, and it was that the program and sobriety were the only way."

—Noelle, a young alcoholic in a

12-step program[13]

BREAKING THE CYCLE OF ABUSE[14]

Alcohol abuse often follows a cycle. A person begins to abuse alcohol, then wants more and more. And the more alcohol a person drinks, the more alcohol it takes to feel the effects. It is a dangerous pattern.

Whether genetic or environmental factors (or both) are at play, people who grow up in a family where alcohol is abused are statistically more likely to become abusers themselves.

It is important to break the cycle of abuse. No matter what statistics say is likely to happen, beginning to abuse alcohol yourself or growing up in a family with rampant alcohol abuse does not have to keep you from living a clean and sober life.

As a preschooler, "Darlene" survived a car accident that killed her mother, older sister, and grandmother. The driver of the other vehicle was drunk. It would not be the last time alcoholism would tear her life and her family apart.

At age fifteen, Darlene met a nineteen-year-old musician who sang away her troubles while he drank away his own. At last, she thought, her long-held dream of love and security would come true. She soon became pregnant, though, and had to drop out of high school.

Darlene's husband drank often, and heavily. "We could never have any alcohol in the apartment without him finishing it," she said. "And when he did, he became angry, abusive, and more jealous, fearing I'd leave him."

Eventually, Darlene gathered the courage to do just that. She broke one cycle of abuse when she took her son and walked out the door. Her husband later spent time in prisons and died before he was fifty.

Darlene returned to school and became a registered nurse. She worked in the mental health field for twenty years. "I observed many teens having experienced their first psychotic or depressive episodes after months or years of 'partying.' They couldn't have known how much alcohol affects our brain chemistry . . . What they come to learn is that although you might feel good when you're doing it, the next day your mood, energy, and ability to enjoy life are down."

Darlene tried to help her own son when he started to abuse alcohol as a teen. "He even prided himself," she said, "on being able to drink more than his buddies before 'feeling it.'" Now he seems to believe some of the lessons his mother taught him. However, this "awakening" did not come before another unplanned pregnancy—from his relationship with a woman who was also a substance abuser. "I pray he will choose not to even try it," Darlene says of her grandson, whose care has fallen largely on her shoulders.

Glossary

Al-Anon—a support group for those whose lives are affected by a friend or relative who is an alcoholic

Alateen—a division of Al-Anon for teens trying to cope with an alcoholic family member or friend

alcohol abuse—the intentional overuse of alcohol, often to the point of drunkenness

Alcoholics Anonymous (AA)—a worldwide self-help group, the largest one for recovering alcoholics

alcoholism—a disease; an addictive dependency on alcohol. It is characterized by craving alcohol, loss of control over drinking, physical dependence and withdrawal symptoms, and alcohol tolerance (the increasing difficulty of becoming drunk). An alcoholic is someone who is addicted to alcohol.

binge drinking—drinking a large amount of alcohol in a short period of time; often defined as five drinks in a row for males and four in a row for females

codependents—people who suffer from an emotional and behavioral condition that affects their ability to form and maintain healthy, mutually satisfying relationships. Codependence often results from growing up in an alcoholic family.

fermentation—the process by which sugars, combined with yeast, are converted to carbon dioxide and alcohol

fetal alcohol syndrome—a condition that can occur in a fetus if a woman drinks alcohol during pregnancy. It can be characterized by abnormal facial features, slow growth, mental retardation, and central nervous system problems, among other birth defects.

Prohibition—the period from 1919 to 1933 in the United States during which the manufacture and sale of alcoholic beverages was forbidden

rehabilitation—treatment to restore an alcohol or drug abuser to good health; often called rehab for short

relapse—an alcoholic's return to former drinking habits after a period of being sober

sober—not drunk

spirits—alcoholic drinks that have been distilled, or purified and condensed, such as whiskey and vodka

temperance—restrained use of or abstinence from alcohol

withdrawal—painful physical and psychological symptoms that occur when a person stops using an addictive substance

Source Notes

Chapter 1

1. Shelly Marshall, *Young, Sober & Free: Experience, Strength, and Hope for Young Adults* (Center City, Minn.: Hazelden, 2003), pp. 13–14.
2. National Institute on Drug Abuse news release, December 17, 1999, http://www.nida.nih.gov/MedAdv/99/NR-1217a.html.
3. Gail B. Stewart, *The Other America: Teen Alcoholics* (San Diego: Lucent Books, Inc., 2000), p. 11.
4. Ibid., p. 12.
5. Center for Disease Control searchable data base, http://apps.nccd.cdc.gov/yrbss/QuestYearTable.asp?path=byHT&ByVar=CI&cat=3&quest=Q40&year=2003&loc=XX
6. Focus Adolescent Services, http://www.focusas.com/Alcohol.html.
7. Lawrence Clayton, Ph.D., *Drug Dangers: Alcohol* (Springfield, N.J.: Enslow Publishers, Inc., 1999), p. 8.
8. Monitoring the Future, http://www.monitoringthefuture.org.
9. Focus Adolescent Services.
10. Michael Windle, "Alcohol Use Among Adolescents and Young Adults," National Institute on Alcohol Abuse and Alcoholism, December 2003, http://www.niaaa.nih.gov/publications/arh27-1/79-86.htm.
11. Focus Adolescent Services.
12. Windle.
13. Ibid.
14. Laurence Pringle, *Drinking: A Risky Business* (New York: Morrow Junior Books, 1997), p. 9.
15. Ibid., p. 10.
16. Linda Raley, Texas Tech University, "Beer History," 1998, http://www.beerhistory.com/library/holdings/raley_timetable.shtml.
17. Pringle, p. 11.
18. Pringle, p. 45.
19. *The Columbia Encyclopedia*, 6th ed., s.v. "alcoholism."
20. National Highway Travel Safety Administration, http://www.cdc.gov/ncipc/factsheets/drving.htm.
21. Ibid.
22. Pringle, p. 80.
23. National Highway Travel Safety Administration, http://www.cdc.gov/ncipc/factsheets/drving.htm.
24. Deborah Straszheim, "The Drinking Age Debate: An Overview," in *Current Controversies: Teens and Alcohol*, ed. James D. Torr, p. 108 (San Diego: Greenhaven Press, Inc., 2002).
25. Ibid.
26. Center for Science in the Public Interest, "Arguments for Lowering the Drinking Age Are Misguided," in *Current Controversies: Teens And Alcohol*, ed. James D. Torr, p. 117 (San Diego: Greenhaven Press, Inc., 2002).
27. Ibid.
28. Casey McCary Bloom, "Drunk Driving Brings a Lifetime of Pain," *University of Florida Independent Alligator*, February 19, 1997, http://www.alligator.org/edit/issues/97-sprg/970219/c02bloom.htm.

Chapter 2

1. Greg Ambrose, "Back on Board," *Honolulu Star-Bulletin*, May 28, 1997, http://starbulletin.com/97/05/28/sports/story2.html.
2. Ibid.
3. Ibid.
4. Bowles Center for Alcohol Studies, University of North Carolina at Chapel Hill, "What Is Alcoholism? What Is Alcohol Abuse?" January 29, 2004, http://www.med.unc.edu/alcohol/ed/abuseism.htm.
5. Charlie Bader, Jaelline Jaffe, and Jeanne Segal, "Alcohol Abuse and Alcoholism: Signs, Effects and Treatment," in *Helpguide*, http://www.helpguide.org/mental/alcohol_abuse_alcoholism_signs_effects_treatment.htm.
6. Wikipedia, http://en.wikipedia.org/wiki/Alcoholism.
7. National Institute on Alcohol Abuse and Alcoholism, "FAQ's on Alcohol Abuse and Alcoholism," updated May 14, 2002, http://www.niaaa.nih.gov/faq/faq.htm.
8. George Washington University Medical Center, "Teens' Alcohol Problems," http://www.alcoholcostcalculator.

org/kids/teens/print-teens.php.

9. National Center on Addiction and Substance Abuse at Columbia University, "Rethinking Rites of Passage: Substance Abuse on America's Campuses," June 1, 1994, http://www.casacolumbia.org/Absolutenm/articlefiles/rethinking_rites_of_passage_6_1_94.pdf.

10. The Marin Institute, "Physiological Effects of Alcohol on Teenagers," 2003, http://www.marininstitute.org/Youth/teen_alcohol_use.htm.

11. National Household Survey on Drug Abuse Report, "Academic Performance and Youth Substance Abuse" (Washington, D.C.: National Household Survey on Drug Abuse, 2002).

12. Stewart, p. 58.

13. National Institute on Alcohol Abuse and Alcoholism database, http://www.niaaa.nih.gov/databases/dkpat3.htm.

14. Stewart, p. 81.

15. Ibid., p. 92.

16. National Survey on Drug Use and Health, "Alcohol Use and Delinquent Behaviors Among Youths," April 1, 2005, http://oas.samhsa.gov/2k5/alcDelinquent/alcDelinquent.htm.

17. Alcohol Policies Project: Center for Science in the Public Interest, "What is the ONDCP National Youth Anti-Drug Media Campaign?" http://www.cspinet.org/booze/ondcp.htm.

18. Barry McCaffrey, testimony before House Government Reform and Oversight Committee, Subcommittee on National Security, International Affairs and Criminal Justice on the ONDCP budget request, March 26, 1998; http://www.cspinet.org/booze/ondcp.htm.

19. Magellan Health Services, "Alcohol Abuse in Adolescents," April 2005, http://www.magellanassist.com/mem/library/healthobserv/apr05_alcoholabuseadol.asp.

20. M. G. Kushner and K. J. Sher, "Comorbidity of Alcohol and Anxiety Disorders Among College Students: Effects of Gender and Family History of Alcoholism," Addictive Behaviors (1993), 18: pp. 543–52.

21. E. Y. Deykin, et al., "Adolescent Depression, Alcohol and Drug Abuse," American Journal of Public Health (1997) 77(2): pp. 178–82.

22. Margaret O. Hyde and John F. Setaro, M.D., Alcohol 101: An Overview for Teens (Brookfield, Conn.: Twenty-First Century Books, 1999), p. 72.

23. Greenblatt.

24. Hyde and Setaro, p. 97.

25. Ibid.

26. National Institute on Alcohol Abuse and Alcoholism, "FAQ's on Alcohol Abuse and Alcoholism," updated May 14, 2002, http://www.niaaa.nih.gov/faq/faq.htm.

27. U.S. Department of Health and Human Services, National Clearinghouse for Drug and Alcohol Information, "A Guide For Teens," http://www.health.org/govpubs/phd688/.

28. Art Pulis, "New Local Company Introduces Youth Addiction Assessment Tool," The Wickenburg (Ariz.) Sun, April 20, 2005, http://www.wickenburgsun.com/articles/2005/04/20/news/news10.txt.

29. Bonnie Delaney, "Kids Get Creative to Talk about Alcohol," Asbury Park (N.J.) Press, March 26, 2005; http://www.app.com/apps/pbcs.dll/article?AID=/20050326/COMMUNITY/503260331/1065.

30. Ibid.

31. Joyesha Chesnick, "Youth Drinking: Tough Nut to Crack," The Arizona Daily Star, December 10, 2004, http://www.dailystar.com/dailystar/relatedarticles/51958.php.

Chapter 3

1. Drug Prevention Network of the Americas, "Parents Who Use Illegal Drugs, Abuse Alcohol and Smoke Endanger Half The Nation's Children," March 29, 2005, http://www.dpna.org/3parentsdrugeffect.htm.

2. Ibid.

3. Marc Alan Schuckit, "Alcoholism Has a Genetic Basis," in Current Controversies: Alcoholism, ed. James D. Torr, p. 73 (San Diego: Greenhaven Press, Inc., 2000).

4. Ibid.
5. Ibid.
6. "U.S., Russian Alcoholics Share Similar Gene," ACER news release, April 16, 2005; http://alcoholism.about.com/od/genetics/a/blacer050416_p.htm.
7. Ibid.
8. Windle, "Parental Drinking Contributes to Teen Alcoholism," in Current Controversies: Teens And Alcohol, ed. James D. Torr, p. 21 (San Diego: Greenhaven Press, Inc., 2002).
9. Clayton, p. 38.
10. Ibid.
11. Ibid.
12. Marilyn McClellan, The Big Deal About Alcohol: What Teens Need to Know About Drinking (Berkeley Heights, N.J.: Enslow Publishers, Inc., 2004), p. 10.
13. Ibid., p. 11.
14. Ibid.
15. Windle, "Parental Drinking Contributes to Teen Alcoholism," pp. 22–23.
16. Ibid., p. 23.
17. Elaine Landau, Issues In Focus: Teenage Drinking (Hillside, N.J.; Enslow Publishers, Inc., 1984), p. 51.
18. U.S. Department of Health and Human Services, National Clearinghouse for Drug and Alcohol Information, "The Role of Parents in Preventing and Addressing Underage Drinking," http://www.health.org/govpubs/RPO991/.
19. Ibid.
20. Drug Prevention Network of the Americas, "Parents Who Use Illegal Drugs, Abuse Alcohol and Smoke Endanger Half The Nation's Children."
21. CASAnet Resources, "National Committee To Prevent Child Abuse Fact Sheet," September 1997; http://www.casanet.org/library/addiction/ncpca.htm.
22. Ibid.
23. Schuckit, "Wives of Alcoholics More Likely to Drink," in Alcoholism: Clinical and Experimental Research; http://alcoholism.about.com/library/weekly/aa020923a.htm.
24. Ibid.
25. Ibid.
26. Ty Tagami, "Mayor Franklin Embraces Her Father's Rocky Past," The Atlanta-Journal Constitution, April 24, 2005, http://www.ajc.com/metro/content/metro/atlanta/0405/24franklin.html.
27. Ibid.
28. Pringle, p. 40.
29. U.S. Department of Health and Human Services, National Clearinghouse for Drug and Alcohol Information, "Fetal Alcohol Syndrome: Incurable and Preventable," http://www.health.org/newsroom/articles/articleDetails.aspx?ID=27.
30. Hyde and Setaro, p. 51.
31. Ibid., p. 53.
32. Ibid., p. 50.
33. McClellan, p. 41.
34. David P. MacKinnon, Rhonda M. Williams-Avery, and Mary Ann Pentz, "Many Teenagers Are Not Aware of the Effects of Drinking on Pregnancy," in Teen Alcoholism: Contemporary Issues Companion, ed. Laura K. Egendorf, p. 58 (San Diego: Greenhaven Press, Inc., 2001).
35. Center for Disease Control, National Center on Birth Defects and Developmental Disabilities, "Fetal Alcohol Information," http://www.cdc.gov/ncbddd/fas/fasask.htm.
36. John Haney, "Knox Co. DA Speaks out on Underage Drinking at Home," WATE Channel 6, Knoxville, Tenn., April 27, 2005, http://www.wate.com/Global/story.asp?S=3272602.
37. Vanessa O'Connell, "Underage Drinking at Home," The Wall Street Journal, September 15, 2004.
38. Michele Oreckin, "You Must Be Over 21 to Drink in This Living Room," Time, April 11, 2005, http://www.time.com/time/magazine/article/0,9171,1047499-1,00.html
39. O'Connell.

Chapter 4

1. PBS, "Binge Drinking," NewsHour with Jim Lehrer transcript, April 10, 2002, http://www.pbs.org/newshour/bb/health/jan-june02/drinking_4-10.html.
2. Ibid.
3. Ibid.
4. Annual Review of Public Health, "College Alcohol Problems Exceed Previous Estimates," March 17, 2005, http://www.nih.gov/news/pr/mar2005/niaaa-17.htm.

5. Ibid.

6. Ibid.

7. Harvard School of Public Health survey, "College Binge Drinking Largely Unabated, Four Years Later," September 10, 1998; http://www.hsph.harvard.edu/cas/Documents/97_survey-pressRelease/.

8. Annual Review of Public Health, "College Alcohol Problems Exceed Previous Estimates."

9. Hyde and Setaro, p. 60.

10. Ibid.

11. PBS, "Q&A: Binge Lessons," NewsHour with Jim Lehrer, June 1999, http://www.pbs.org/newshour/bb/health/jan-june99/qa_casa.html.

12. Hyde and Setaro, p. 61.

13. PBS, "Q&A: Binge Lessons," NewsHour with Jim Lehrer.

14. NIAAA Report, "High-Risk Drinking in College," http://www.collegedrinkingprevention.gov/Reports/Panel01/HighRisk_03.aspx.

15. About.com, "Students Find Easy Access to Alcohol," June 23, 2000, http://alcoholism.about.com/cs/college/a/aa000623a.htm

16. Ibid.

17. American Council on Alcoholism, "College Drinking," http://www.aca-usa.org/college.htm.

18. Hyde and Setaro, p. 62.

19. CNN, "Study: Underage Drinkers Starting at Earlier Age," February 27, 2002, http://archives.cnn.com/2002/HEALTH/parenting/02/26/teen.drinking/.

20. Hyde and Setaro, p. 62.

21. Ibid.

22. Mary Carmichael, "Driving Kids from Drink," Newsweek, 2005, http://www.msnbc.msn.com/id/5626597/site/newsweek/.

23. Ibid.

24. Andrew Grossman, "Social Norms: Peer Pressure Redux," The Dartmouth Review, November 5, 1999, http://www.dartreview.com/issues/11.5.99/socialnorms.html.

25. Ibid.

26. Tom Gibb, "A Senior at Penn State Almost Dies Celebrating His Birthday with 21 Drinks," Pittsburgh Post-Gazette, August 27, 1999; http://www.post-gazette.com/regionstate/19990827drunk2.asp.

27. Karen Lee Scrivo, "How Colleges Have Responded to Teenage Drinking," in Teen Alcoholism: Contemporary Issues Companion, ed. Laura K. Egendorf, pp. 100–101 (San Diego: Greenhaven Press, Inc., 2001).

28. U.S. Department of Health and Human Services, National Clearinghouse for Drug and Alcohol Information, "College and University Students," http://www.health.org/govpubs/phd627/college.aspx.

29. Ibid., p. 101.

30. Ibid.

31. Ed Cohen, "Sobering Debate," Notre Dame Magazine, Summer 2002; http://www.nd.edu/~ndmag/su2002/alcohol.html.

32. Ibid.

33. Susan Okie, "Drinking Lessons," The Washington Post, April 16, 2002; http://www.washingtonpost.com/ac2/wp-dyn?pagename=article&node=&contentId=A54768-2002Apr15&notFound=true.

34. Harvard School of Public Health survey.

35. Ibid.

36. Okie.

37. PRNewswire, "Teens Report Pressure to Engage in High-Risk Behaviors on Prom and Graduation Nights, Impacting Driving Safety," May 10, 2005, http://www.prnewswire.com/cgi-bin/stories.pl?ACCT=109&STORY=/www/story/05-10-2005/0003592281&EDATE=.

38. Ibid.

39. Lisa Renze-Rhodes, "Carmel Is Latest to Test for Pre-prom Alcohol Use," The Indianapolis Star, March 5, 2005.

40. National Crime Prevention Council: "Strategy: Prom-Time Drinking and Driving Prevention Programs," http://www.ncpc.org/ncpc/ncpc/?pg=2088-8800.

Chapter 5

1. James Gilden, "A Toast to the Under-21 Crowd," Chicago Tribune, April 17, 2005; http://www.chicagotribune.com/travel/chi-g6e1rh1p4.21apr17,1,3481277.story?coll=chi-travel-hed&ctrack=1&cset=true.

2. David J. Hanson, "Health Issues: Alcohol, Tradition and Health," SUNY Potsdam, http://www2.potsdam.edu/alcohol-info/HealthIssues/1043186392.html.

3. Gilden.

4. Hanson.

5. Gilden.

6. Social Issues Research Centre, "Social and Cultural Aspects of Drinking," Oxford, UK, http://www.sirc.org/publik/drinking3.html.

7. Ibid.

8. MSN Encarta Encyclopedia, "alcoholism," http://encarta.msn.com/encyclopedia_761552168/Alcoholism.html.

9. David J. Hanson, "It's Better to Teach Safe Use of Alcohol," SUNY Potsdam, http://www2.potsdam.edu/alcohol-info/YouthIssues/1044361545.html.

10. Charles Robinson, "Intoxicated State," The State News, November 17, 1998; http://www.statenews.com/alcohol/windsor1.html.

11. Ibid.

12. Dwight B. Heath, "American Attitudes toward Alcohol Lead to Underage Drinking," in Teen Alcoholism: Contemporary Issues Companion, ed. Laura K. Egendorf, p. 26 (San Diego: Greenhaven Press, Inc., 2001).

13. L. Leiber, "Commercial and Character Slogan Recall by Children Aged 9 to 11 Years: Budweiser Frogs versus Bugs Bunny" (Berkeley: Center on Alcohol Advertising, 1996), http://camy.org/factsheets/index.php?FactsheetID=1.

14. C. F. Garfield, P. J. Chung, and P. J. Rathouz, "Alcohol Advertising in Magazines and Youth Readership," The Journal of the American Medical Association 289, no. 18 (May 14, 2003): pp. 2424–29.

15. Henry Saffer, "Alcohol Advertising and Youth," NIAAA Report: Journal of Studies on Alcohol, http://www.collegedrinkingprevention.gov/Reports/Journal/saffer.aspx.

16. About.com, "Super Bowl Booze Ads Target Kids," January 2, 2005, http://alcoholism.about.com/library/weekly/aa010205a.htm.

17. B. Horovitz and M. Wells, "Ads for Adult Vices Big Hit with Teens," USA Today, January 31, 1997, p. 1A.

18. Joel W. Grube, "Alcohol Advertising: A Study of Children and Adolescents," Prevention Research Center of the Pacific Institute for Research and Evaluation, http://www.prev.org/prc/prc_text_grube_aasca.html.

19. Ibid.

20. Thomas N. Robinson, Helen L. Chen and Joel D. Killen, "Television and Music Video Exposure and Risk of Adolescent Alcohol Use," Pediatrics In Review, November 1998, http://pediatrics.aappublications.org/cgi/content/full/102/5/e54.

21. Ibid.

22. Ibid.

23. American Medical News, "AMA Condemns NASCAR Decision to Allow Liquor Sponsorship," December 13, 2004, http://www.ama-assn.org/amednews/2004/12/13/hlbf1213.htm.

24. The Associated Press, "NASCAR Lifts Ban on Liquor Sponsorship," Columbia Daily Tribune, http://www.showmenews.com/2004/Nov/20041111Spor048.asp.

25. PBS, "NBC to Stop Airing Liquor Ads," Online NewsHour, March 20, 2002; http://www.pbs.org/newshour/media/media_watch/jan-june02/nbc_3-20.html.

26. Join Together, "Liquor Industry Gets Aggressive with Advertising," May 26, 2004; http://www.jointogether.org/sa/news/summaries/reader/0%2C1854%2C571115%2C00.html.

Chapter 6

1. Al-Anon/Alateen official Web site, http://www.al-anon.alateen.org/prelease/prparents.html.

2. Ibid.

3. Margi Trapani, Inside a Support Group: Help for Teenage Children of Alcoholics (New York: The Rosen Publishing Group, Inc., 1997), pp. 43–44.

4. Ibid.

5. MADD official Web site, "Really MADD: Looking Back at 20 Years," spring 2000, http://www.madd.org/aboutus/0,1056,1686,00.html.

6. Ibid.
7. Ibid.
8. SADD official Web site, *http://www. saddonline.com/history.htm.*
9. Marshall, p. 69.
10. Robert Zimmerman, "Alcoholics Anonymous is Effective," in *Current Controversies: Alcoholism,* ed. James D. Torr, p. 92 (San Diego: Greenhaven Press, Inc., 2000).
11. Ibid.
12. Marshall, p. 69.
13. Marshall, p. 134.
14. Author interview, May 12–13, 2005.

To Find Out More

BOOKS

Egendorf, Laura K., ed. *Teen Alcoholism: Contemporary Issues Companion.* San Diego: Greenhaven Press, 2001.

Hyde, Margaret O., and John F. Setaro, MD. *Alcohol 101: An Overview for Teens.* Brookfield, Conn.: Twenty-First Century Books, 1999.

Kulp, Liz, and Jodee Kulp. *The Best I Can Be: Living with Fetal Alcohol Syndrome-Effects.* Brooklyn Park, Minn.: Better Endings New Beginnings, 2000.

Marshall, Shelly. *Young, Sober & Free: Experience, Strength, and Hope for Young Adults.* Center City, Minn.: Hazelden, 2003.

McClellan, Marilyn. *The Big Deal about Alcohol: What Teens Need to Know about Drinking.* Berkeley Heights, N.J.: Enslow Publishers, 2004.

Miller, Susan B. *When Parents Have Problems: A Book for Teens and Older Children with an Abusive, Alcoholic, or Mentally Ill Parent.* Springfield, Ill.: Charles C. Thomas, 1995.

Packer, Alex J. *Highs! Over 150 Ways to Feel Really, Really Good . . . Without Alcohol or Other Drugs.* Minneapolis: Free Spirit Publishing, 2000.

Pringle, Laurence. *Drinking: A Risky Business*. New York: Morrow Junior Books, 1997.

Rosengren, John. *Big Book Unplugged: A Young Person's Guide to Alcoholics Anonymous*. Center City, Minn.: Hazelden, 2003.

Stewart, Gail B. *Teen Alcoholics*. San Diego: Lucent Books, 2000.

Zailckas, Koren. *Smashed: Story of a Drunken Girlhood*. New York: Viking Adult, 2005.

Multimedia Resources

Alcohol–Brain Under the Influence. Tapeworm, 1998.

Reel Life Teens: Alcohol. TMW/Media Group, 2002.

Teens, Alcohol & Tobacco. American Portrait, 2002.

Online Sites

American Council on Alcoholism (ACA)
   http://www.aca-usa.org
Focus Adolescent Services (FocusAS)
   http://www.focusas.com
National Council on Alcoholism and
   Drug Dependence (NCADD)
   http://www.ncadd.org
National Institute on Drug Abuse (NIDA)
   http://www.nida.nih.gov
National Institute on Alcohol Abuse
   and Alcoholism (NIAAA)
   http://www.niaaa.nih.gov

Organizations

Al-Anon/Alateen
1600 Corporate Landing Parkway
Virginia Beach, VA 23454
757-563-1600
E-mail: wso@al-anon.org
http://www.al-anon.alateen.org
Al-Anon, which includes Alateen for younger members, offers help to
families and friends of alcoholics. The organization publishes books,
pamphlets, service materials, and a monthly magazine, *The Forum*.

Alcoholics Anonymous (AA)

Grand Central Station
PO Box 459
New York, NY 10163
http://www.aa.org
AA offers help to more than 2 million members worldwide, and the only requirement for membership is a desire to stop drinking. AA provides a literature catalog and publishes a monthly journal, A.A. Grapevine.

Mothers Against Drunk Driving (MADD)

511 E. John Carpenter Freeway, Suite 700
Irving, TX 75062
800-GET-MADD
http://www.madd.org
MADD lobbies for strict laws and aggressive enforcement against those who endanger their own lives and the lives of others by drinking and driving.

Students Against Destructive Decisions (SADD)

255 Main Street
Marlborough, MA 01752
877-SADD-INC
E-mail: info@sadd.org
http://www.sadd.org
This organization addresses important issues with fellow students, including underage drinking, drunk driving, drug use, and violence. The SADD Web site offers free access to a newsletter and brochures.

Index

About the Author

A veteran editor of history and sports books, David Aretha has authored more than twenty books for young people. Five of those books have focused on the dangers of substance abuse, including cocaine, methamphetamine, party drugs, inhalants, and steroids.